PHRASAL VERBS *in context*

PETER DAINTY

PHOENIX
ELT

incorporating
HALL MACMILLAN

Published 1995 by
Phoenix ELT
Campus 400, Spring Way
Maylands Avenue, Hemel Hempstead
Hertfordshire, HP2 7EZ
A division of Prentice Hall International

First published 1991 by Macmillan Publishers Ltd

Illustration by Peter Kent
Produced by AMR

Printed and bound in Malaysia

A catalogue record for this book is available from the British Library

ISBN 0 13–402819–8

7   6   5   4   3

99   98   97   96   95

A29213

CONTENTS

INTRODUCTION

This book offers you a new method for learning phrasal verbs such as 'put on', 'take off', 'give up' and 'look for'.

It starts with a specially written cartoon story in which **325** common phrasal verbs are introduced in a tale of adventure, love, money, crime, honour and a blue Rolls Royce. To help you recognise these different verb-preposition forms and bring them into your active vocabulary, there are follow-up exercises and detailed grammar notes.

Then – in Part Two – there is an extended blank-filling revision exercise based on the cartoon.

Part Three has the answers for all the exercises and a full alphabetical listing of the phrasal verbs, cross-referenced to the original text.

If you learn some of the story by heart and do all the follow-up exercises, you should find that these 325 phrasal verbs can become a part of your everyday language as you develop a more natural and more instinctive command of English.

But now, as Sir Gerald Prescott would say, 'Let's go through the whole story right from the start'...

CHAPTER ONE

ON A COLD NOVEMBER EVENING MANY YEARS AGO, ANGUS MACPHERSON (CHIEF GUARD AT THE NEWTOWN PRISON) YAWNED AND CLOSED HIS EYES.

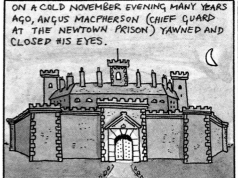

ANGUS HAD HAD A LONG AND TIRING DAY AND NOW, AS THE CLOCK STRUCK 11, THE THREE PLATEFULS OF SPAGHETTI BOLOGNESE HE'D ENJOYED AT DINNER WERE PULLING HIM TOWARDS THE DEEPEST OF DEEP SLEEPS.

I'll just have a little nap. All the cells are locked and everything's quiet. I'm sure nobody will mind if I nod off for a while.

ANGUS STRETCHED OUT ON A WOODEN BENCH AND TRIED TO RELAX. BUT, FOR SOME REASON, HE COULDN'T GET OFF TO SLEEP. THEN HE HAD AN IDEA.

I know what the trouble is. It's this belt of mine. It's much too tight.

HE ROLLED OVER, TOOK OFF THE BELT AND DROPPED IT ON TO THE FLOOR.

A FEW MINUTES LATER THE STONE CORRIDORS ECHOED TO ANGUS MACPHERSON'S UNMISTAKEABLE SNORE.

IN THE DARKNESS OF CELL 269, FREDERICK CARRUTHERS (A BANK MANAGER WHO HAD LENT HIMSELF £250,000) WAS PLANNING HIS ESCAPE.

If I could get the keys off MacPherson's belt, I could slip out through the side door, run across the yard, jump over the prison wall and be back home for breakfast.

But how do I do it?

JUST THEN HE CAUGHT SIGHT OF ANGUS' BELT LYING ON THE FLOOR.

The keys! He's just dropped the belt with the keys. This is too good to be true.

HE TIPTOED TO THE FRONT OF THE CELL AND LOOKED AROUND. THERE WAS NO ONE ABOUT. HE TOOK A DEEP BREATH...

269

Carruthers. F.
3 years
Robbery

...AND THEN, SOFTLY AND SLOWLY, HE STRETCHED OUT HIS HAND, PICKED UP THE BELT AND LIFTED IT BACK THROUGH THE BARS...

Practice

1 Complete the following sentences using one of the words below.

breakfast	floor	keys	b~~e~~lt	door
bars	wall	cell	breath	yard

1 He rolled over, took off the _____*belt*_____ .

2 ...and dropped it onto the _____ .

3 If I could get the _____ off Macpherson's belt,

4 ...I could slip out through the side _____ ,

5 ...run across the _____ ,

6 ...jump over the prison _____

7 ...and be back home for _____ .

8 He tiptoed to the front of the _____ and looked around.

9 There was no one about. He took a deep _____ ,

10 ....picked up the belt and lifted it back through the _____ .

2 Complete the following sentences using one of the prepositions below.

off	out	up	~~off~~	over
about	around	across	over	to

1 For some reason, he couldn't get _____*off*_____ to sleep.

2 He rolled _____ , took off the belt and dropped it onto the floor.

3 A few minutes later, the stone corridors echoed _____ the sound of Angus Macpherson's unmistakable snore.

4 If I could get the keys _____ Macpherson's belt,

5 I could slip _____ through the side door,

6 ...run _____ the yard,

7 ...jump _____ the prison wall and be back home for breakfast.

8 He tiptoed to the front of the cell and looked _____ .

9 There was no one _____ .

10 He picked _____ the belt and lifted it back through the bars.

Notes

1 *a nap* = a short, light sleep

2 *to nod off* = to fall asleep gradually

3 When talking about clothes, *to take off* is the opposite of *to put on*.

'Angus...took off the belt and dropped it onto the floor.' (Chapter One)

'She put on her coat.' (Chapter Three)

4 Two common meanings of *slip* are...

    a to move quietly or secretly, trying not to be seen

       'I could slip out through the side door...' (Chapter One)

       'But whenever my father's back was turned, I would slip out of the house and go and meet Gerald secretly.' (Chapter Eight)

    and

    b to fall or nearly fall

       ◆ She slipped on a banana skin and sprained her ankle.

5 Notice the difference between *to jump over*, *to jump onto* and *to jump off*...

    a 'I could slip out through the side door, run across the yard, jump over the prison wall and be back home for breakfast.' (Chapter One)

    and

    b 'Frederick had...jumped onto a train that was slowing down in front of a set of signals, run down the corridor to avoid the ticket collector and then jumped off again as the train pulled into a station.' (Chapter Five)

6 'There was no one about' = Nobody else was there

Compare ...

    'Lady Prescott got out of the car and looked around. There was no one else about.' (Chapter Fourteen)

and

    'Frederick turned his face and looked out at Crawford Street. There were now lots of people about. It was half past three and the local school had just broken up for the day.' (Chapter Twelve)

Note that *to look around* generally has the idea of looking on all sides, while *to look round* suggests that the person turns to look at something they couldn't see before.

round can also be an informal word for *around*.

CHAPTER TWO

Practice

3 Complete the following sentences using one of the words below.

lunchbreak	door	desk	tears	cell
handkerchief	keys	*Times*	~~belt~~	minutes

1 He stood up and looked for his ____*belt*____.

2 Sir Gerald Prescott was sitting at his _____ reading *The Times*.

3 He's broken out of his _____ and run away.

4 I nodded off for a few _____.

5 Carruthers picked up the belt and took off one of the _____.

6 He opened his cell and slipped out through the side _____.

7 Sir Gerald tore up his _____

8 ...and burst into _____.

9 Angus took a _____ out of his pocket.

10 I'll give up my _____ and go out and look for him and find out where he is...

4 Complete the following sentences using one of the prepositions below.

out	away	off	with	at
to	off	up	out	~~for~~

1 He stood up and looked ____*for*____ his belt.

2 Sir Gerald was sitting _____ his desk reading *The Times*.

3 Angus rushed in, his red face covered _____ sweat.

4 He's broken _____ of his cell

5 ...and run _____!

6 I nodded _____ for a few minutes.

7 Sir Gerald tore _____ his *Times* and burst into tears.

8 Angus took a handkerchief _____ of his pocket

9 ...and handed it _____ Sir Gerald.

10 I shouldn't have taken _____ my belt and nodded off like that.

Notes

1 *dawn* can be a noun ('Dawn broke over Newtown Prison') and a verb ('the...truth dawned on him').

2 There are many phrasal verbs with *look*. Among the most common are...

to look for = to try to find
to look at = to see; to examine
to look after = to take care of

'He stood up and looked for his belt.' (Chapter Two)
'I looked at the cheque. My head was spinning.' (Chapter Eleven)

'She looks after sick children.' (Chapter Ten)

3 *to work (something) out* = to solve (a problem, puzzle, mystery, etc.)

4 *to let in* (= to allow to enter) is the opposite of *to let out* (= to allow to leave).

'Governor! Governor! Let me in! Let me in!' (Chapter Two)

'When he came to the prison gates, he knocked on the front door and the night guard let him in.' (Chapter Fifteen)

'There was no need for you to run off like that. They were going to let you out anyway.' (Chapter Thirteen)

5 Note the difference between *to sit at, to sit back, to sit down, to sit in* and *to sit up.*

'Sir Gerald was sitting at his desk reading *The Times.*' (Chapter Two)

'Frederick sat back and just watched the volcano erupt.' (Chapter Seven)

'Angus sat down and took a deep breath.' (Chapter Two)

'Here he was, sitting in a Rolls Royce driven by the wife of the governor of the prison he'd just escaped from.' (Chapter Seven)

'He was so ill that he couldn't sit up in bed properly.' (Chapter Ten)

6 *to calm down* = to relax

'Now calm down. And go through the whole story right from the start.' (Chapter Two)

'By the time they arrived at the outskirts of Birmingham, Lady Prescott had calmed down a little and Frederick was feeling a bit more relaxed.' (Chapter Eight)

7 *to make up for (something)* = to compensate for (something)

'I'll make up for it. I'll give up my lunchbreak and go out and look for him and find out where he is.' (Chapter Two)

'And, now, there was so much to say, so much to do. So much lost time to make up for.' (Chapter Fourteen)

CHAPTER THREE

Practice

5

coat	door	pounds	patience	marriage
tears	coat	prisoners	breakdown	nonsense

1 Lady Prescott took off her _____.

2 Yet another of my _____ has run away.

3 And with that he burst into _____ again.

4 I've had enough of all this _____.

5 I'm leaving you, Gerald! I'm going to break up our _____ and run away.

6 She put on her _____.

7 I'll have a nervous _____.

8 I'm going to walk out of that _____.

9 The cost of repairing the damage could run into hundreds of _____.

10 I've run out of _____, Gerald.

6

up	with	up	out	on
into	of	away	off	about

1 She took _____ her coat.

2 Why don't you grow _____?

3 I can't help it. Yet another of my prisoners has run _____.

4 And with that he burst _____ tears again.

5 I've had enough _____ all this nonsense.

6 I'm not going to put up _____ it any longer.

7 I'm leaving you, Gerald! I'm going to break _____ our marriage.

8 She put _____ her coat.

9 Money! Money! Money! That's all you care _____!

10 I've run _____ of patience, Gerald.

Notes

1 *Grow up!* = Stop behaving like a child!

2 *to put up with* = to tolerate

'I'm not going to put up with it any longer.' (Chapter Three)

'...and you've put up with all my complaints about Sir Gerald.' (Chapter Nine)

3 A *run-down* area is poor, dirty and in decline.

4 *to break up* (= to finish) can be used to describe the end of a relationship, a marriage, a school day and a school term.

'I'm going to break up our marriage and run away to a run-down area of Birmingham.' (Chapter Three)

'There were now lots of people about. It was half past three and the local school had just broken up for the day.' (Chapter Twelve)

5 The noun *breakdown* and the phrasal verb *to break down* can be used to describe people or machines.

'I'll have a nervous breakdown.' (Chapter Three)

'The bus broke down and all the passengers had to get off and walk.' (Chapter Nine)

6 You can also *run out of* time, money, food and ideas.

Chapter Four

Practice

7

chair	room	smoking	tears	jogging
weight	tie	handkerchief	women	dinner

1 The prison governor knelt down and burst into _____.

2 I've been working too hard and putting on _____.

3 I'll take up _____ and take off weight!

4 I'll give up _____

5 ...and wash up after _____!

6 Lady Prescott knocked over a _____

7 ...and stormed out of the _____.

8 The prison governor sat down and straightened his _____.

9 I can't understand _____, Angus. I just can't make them out.

10 Sir Gerald took a _____ out of his pocket.

8

out	down	up	out	round
away	after	over	out	on

1 I've been working too hard and putting _____ weight.

2 You can't walk _____ on me like this.

3 If you went _____ I'd go to pieces.

4 Lady Prescott turned _____,

5 ...knocked _____ a chair,

6 ...and stormed _____ of the room.

7 Shall I go _____ her?

8 The prison governor sat _____ and straightened his tie.

9 She blows _____ all the time.

10 I can't understand women, Angus. I just can't make them

_____.

Notes

1 *down* often means 'to the ground' or 'to the floor'.

'The prison governor knelt down and burst into tears.' (Chapter Four)

'They promise to pull down the terraced housing and build some new flats.' (Chapter Eight)

'I don't want them tearing down my childhood. They should leave my home alone.' (Chapter Eight)

◆ He fell down the stairs and twisted his ankle.

◆ The boxer was knocked down in the fourth round.

◆ They shot down three enemy planes.

2 When talking about weight, a handbrake or a seat belt, *to put on* is the opposite of *to take off*.

'I've been working too hard and putting on weight.' (Chapter Four)

♦ That new diet is amazing! I've taken off six kilos in three days.

'Lady Prescott put on the handbrake...' (Chapter Eight)

'The woman got in, put on her seat belt, took off the handbrake...' (Chapter Six)

'Frederick took off his seat belt and tried to get out of the car.' (Chapter Twelve)

3 *to walk out on* = to abandon

4 *to take up* = to start to do (a new job, a new sport, etc.)

'I'll take up jogging and take off weight!' (Chapter Four)

'"And if I was to take up this new challenge," Frederick said, "you'd expect me to keep quiet about the events of two years ago."' (Chapter Thirteen)

5 'Storming out of a room' is more dramatic than 'walking out of a room'.

6 *to go after* = to run after = to follow

'Shall I go after her?' (Chapter Four)

'If you run away, I'll run after you.' (Chapter Three)

7 *to make up your mind* = to make a decision

'She's made up her mind to run away to a run-down area of Birmingham.' (Chapter Four)

'It didn't take me long to make up my mind!' (Chapter Eight)

8 'I don't know what's got into her' = I don't understand why she is acting so strangely

9 *to blow up* = to lose your temper, to get angry suddenly

10 *to make (someone) out* = to understand (someone); to appreciate what drives or motivates another person

Chapter Five

BY THE TIME THAT LADY PRESCOTT HAD STORMED OUT OF THE OFFICE, AND SIR GERALD HAD STRAIGHTENED HIS TIE, AND ANGUS HAD COME OUT FROM BEHIND THE ARMCHAIR, FREDERICK CARRUTHERS WAS WELL ON HIS WAY HOME.

AFTER HE HAD SLIPPED OUT THROUGH THE SIDE DOOR,

FREDERICK HAD RUN ACROSS THE PRISON YARD,

CLIMBED OVER A WALL

AND RUN OFF INTO THE NIGHT.

HAVING CROSSED THE MAIN ROAD THAT LINKS NEWTOWN TO OLDTOWN,

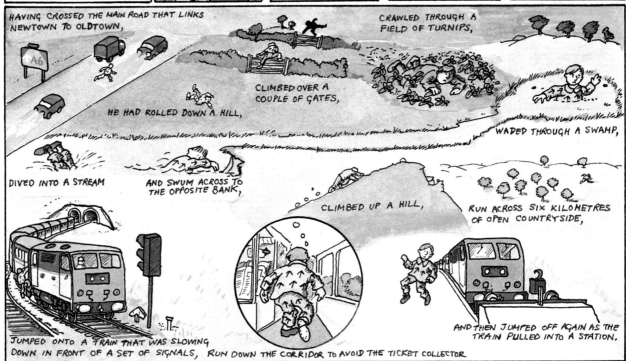

HE HAD ROLLED DOWN A HILL,

CLIMBED OVER A COUPLE OF GATES,

CRAWLED THROUGH A FIELD OF TURNIPS,

WADED THROUGH A SWAMP,

DIVED INTO A STREAM

AND SWUM ACROSS TO THE OPPOSITE BANK,

CLIMBED UP A HILL,

RUN ACROSS SIX KILOMETRES OF OPEN COUNTRYSIDE,

AND THEN JUMPED OFF AGAIN AS THE TRAIN PULLED INTO A STATION.

JUMPED ONTO A TRAIN THAT WAS SLOWING DOWN IN FRONT OF A SET OF SIGNALS,

RUN DOWN THE CORRIDOR TO AVOID THE TICKET COLLECTOR

WHILE THE OTHER PASSENGERS WERE GETTING OFF THE TRAIN, FREDERICK HAD SLIPPED THROUGH THE TICKET BARRIER BY SHOWING HIS PRISON IDENTIFICATION BADGE.

> I'm a train engineer. Let me through! Let me through!

THEN HE'D ELBOWED HIS WAY THROUGH A GROUP OF TOURISTS,

> **#**!!   **#*!**   **#*!**!!

RUSHED DOWN A FLIGHT OF STEPS,

RUN THROUGH A SUBWAY TUNNEL

AND, FINALLY, ENDED UP STANDING OUTSIDE A CAFE AT A LAY-BY

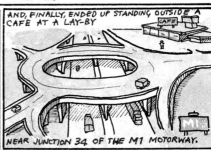

NEAR JUNCTION 34 OF THE M1 MOTORWAY.

IT WAS AT THIS MOMENT THAT HIS PROBLEMS REALLY BEGAN. FREDERICK HAD BEEN RUSHING, ROLLING, RUNNING, JUMPING, CLIMBING, CRAWLING, WADING AND SWIMMING FOR SEVERAL HOURS NOW AND THE LAST MEAL HE'D HAD WAS THREE BISCUITS AND A GLASS OF WATER BEFORE ANGUS HAD TURNED OUT THE LIGHT IN HIS CELL. HIS EXHAUSTED BODY WAS BEGINNING TO COMPLAIN.

HIS STOMACH WAS CRYING OUT FOR FOOD AND HIS THROAT FELT LIKE SANDPAPER. BUT WHAT COULD HE DO? PRISONERS DON'T CARRY MONEY AND HE DIDN'T HAVE A PENNY ON HIM.

FREDERICK LOOKED THROUGH THE WINDOWS OF THE CAFE AND FOR THE NEXT FEW MINUTES HE WENT THROUGH A DREADFUL TORTURE.

> What have I done to deserve this? Here am I — with my stomach rumbling and my throat parched and I can't even afford a cup of tea! How did I get into this mess? And, more to the point, how do I get out of it?

THESE WERE THE THOUGHTS RUNNING THROUGH FREDERICK CARRUTHERS' TROUBLED MIND AS A BLUE ROLLS ROYCE PULLED INTO THE LAY-BY AND GLIDED TO A HALT.

Practice

9 Revision Exercise

In Chapters One to Five, who...

	Angus	Sir Gerald	Lady Prescott	Frederick Carruthers
1 ...nodded off?	✓			
2 ...took off his belt?				
3 ...was sitting at his desk?				
4 ...rushed in?				
5 ...sat down?				
6 ...slipped out through the side door?				
7 ...tore up his *Times*?				
8 ...burst into tears?				
9 ...took off her coat?				
10 ...ran out of patience?				
11 ...knelt down?				
12 ...turned round?				
13 ...blows up all the time?				
14 ...can't make women out?				
15 ...crawled through a field of turnips?				
16 ...jumped off a train?				
17 ...ran across six kilometres of open countryside?				
18 ...elbowed his way through a group of tourists?				
19 ...ended up standing outside a café?				
20 ...pulled into a lay-by?				

Notes

1 In this sense, *to run off* and *to run away* have the same meaning.

2 *to crawl* = to move on all fours

3 The literal meaning of *to wade through* is 'to walk through water or mud that is knee or chest high'.
For this reason, storks and flamingoes are known as *wading birds*.

to wade through can also be used metaphorically with the sense of 'having to read lots of boring information'.

◆ I had to wade through 500 pages of detailed text before I found what I was looking for.

4 *to slow down* = to reduce your speed gradually

5 For buses, trains and planes, *to get on* is the opposite of *to get off.*

'While the other passengers were getting off the train...' (Chapter Five)

'The bus broke down and all the passengers had to get off and walk.' (Chapter Nine)

6 Compare...

'Frederick ended up standing outside a café at a lay-by near Junction 34 of the M1 motorway.' (Chapter Five)

'If she found out that he was a convict on the run, perhaps she'd turn him in and then he might end up in cell 269 again.' (Chapter Ten)

'How could a good man end up like this?' (Chapter Twelve)

7 *out* can mean 'loudly', 'openly', 'publicly', 'noisily' or 'angrily'.

'His stomach was crying out for food.' (Chapter Five)

◆ They shouted out the names...
◆ He spoke out against injustice...
◆ They called out the winning numbers...

8 Compare *to go through* and *to go through with.*

a *to go through* = to suffer

'For the next few minutes, he went through a dreadful torture.' (Chapter Five)

'For the next few months, we went through a really bad patch.' (Chapter Nine)

b *to go through with (something)* = to do (something) even though you know it will be difficult, frustrating or painful

'I've decided to go through with the trial.' (Chapter Eleven)

9 Compare...

'These were the thoughts running through Frederick Carruthers' troubled mind as a blue Rolls Royce pulled into the lay-by and glided to a halt.' (Chapter Five)

and

'Through Frederick's mind went a simple formula – changing a wheel is work. Work brings money. Money brings food.' (Chapter Six)

CHAPTER SIX

Practice

10

window	mirror	handbrake	cloth	lay-by
jacket	hand	tyre	glass	seat belt

1 The driver wound down her _____ and leaned across.

2 Frederick bent down and ran his hand over the _____.

3 He pulled a large piece of _____ out of the wheel and held it up.

4 He took off his _____.

5 Frederick nodded, smiled and held out his _____.

6 He wiped his hands on a _____.

7 The woman put on her _____,

8 ...took off the _____,

9 ...looked in the rear-view _____,

10 ...and pulled gently out of the _____.

11

out	out	on	on	up
off	off	in	over	onto

1 Frederick bent down and ran his hand _____ the tyre.

2 Then he pulled a large piece of glass _____ of the wheel

3 ...and held it _____.

4 Frederick nodded, smiled and held _____ his hand.

5 Perhaps I can drop you _____ somewhere along the way.

6 But then it suddenly dawned _____ Frederick that the offer of a free ride in a Rolls Royce far away from Newtown might be quite a good idea.

7 The woman got _____,

8 ...put _____ her seat belt,

9 ...took _____ the handbrake,

10 ...and then – with a sudden burst of speed – they roared _____ the M1 motorway like a bullet from a gun.

Notes

1 Compare *to hold up* (= vertical) and *to hold out* (= horizontal).

'Then he pulled a large piece of glass out of the wheel and held it up.' (Chapter Six)

'I held up my hand and the man from the bank stopped talking.' (Chapter Eleven)

'Frederick nodded, smiled and held out his hand.' (Chapter Six)

2 *up* can mean...

a higher

'He...jacked up the car...' (Chapter Six)

'She picked up the phone again.' (Chapter Twelve)

b to the end

'By that summer, I'd managed to save up a quarter of a million pounds. (Chapter Eleven)

'Frederick drank up his coffee...' (Chapter Twelve)

and

c thinking creatively or imaginatively

'At first, I couldn't think what to do. But then – all of a sudden – I came up with an idea.' (Chapter Ten)

'But – each week – I made up some new story to explain the cheques away.' (Chapter Eleven)

3 *to drop (someone) off* is the opposite of *to pick (someone) up.*

'Perhaps I could drop you off somewhere along the way.' (Chapter Six)

'...he'd come and pick me up when the classes were over.' (Chapter Eight)

4 *to let (someone) down* = to disappoint (someone), to break a promise

'Frederick's face dropped. He'd been expecting money or food and he felt a bit let down.' (Chapter Six)

'I can't let the children down.' (Chapter Eleven)

5 'it suddenly dawned on him that' = he suddenly realised that

6 When talking about cars, vans or lorries, *to get into* is the opposite of *to get out of.*

'He wiped his hands on a cloth and got into the car.' (Chapter Six)

'Frederick took off his seat belt and tried to get out of the car.' (Chapter Twelve)

7 *to pull out of* (= to leave) a lay-by, station, etc. is the opposite of *to pull into* (= to enter) a lay-by, station, etc.

'The woman got in, put on her seat belt, took off the handbrake, put the car into first gear, looked in the rear-view mirror, and pulled gently out of the lay-by.' (Chapter Six)

'...and then jumped off again as the train pulled into a station.' (Chapter Five)

8 *roar* (the noun) and *to roar* (the verb) are used to describe the sound made by crowds, lions, cars, trains and planes.

'And then – with a sudden burst of speed – they roared onto the M1 motorway like a bullet from a gun.' (Chapter Six)

'The driver put her foot down and the blue Rolls Royce roared on.' (Chapter Seven)

CHAPTER SEVEN

THE BLUE ROLLS ROYCE SPED ON DOWN THE M1.

The steering's fine now. I'm very grateful to you Mr...er...

Carruthers, Frederick Carruthers.

Now that name rings a bell. I'm sure I've come across it somewhere before. But I can't quite place it. And so, tell me Mr Carruthers, what do you do?

FREDERICK PAUSED. HE LOOKED OUT OF THE WINDOW AND WAVED HIS HAND IN A RATHER VAGUE WAY.

I...er...I'm in prisons.

Well I never! Isn't that a coincidence! So is my husband. Perhaps you've heard of him. His name is Sir Gerald Prescott.

FREDERICK SANK LOWER IN HIS SEAT. A COLD SHIVER RAN DOWN HIS SPINE.

Your husband is Sir Gerald Prescott? The Governor of Newtown Jail?

That's right! Do you know him?

Er...not personally. But I...em... know of him... he has quite a reputation in my field.

Does he? Does he indeed? Well I'm sure it's a reputation for childish, incompetent stupidity! My husband has the intelligence of a pineapple and the imagination of a do-nut.

LADY PRESCOTT'S VOICE GREW LOUDER AS SHE WARMED TO HER SUBJECT.

Sir Gerald is the weakest, the stupidest, the meanest and the most selfish man to walk this earth.

FREDERICK WANTED TO MOVE ON TO ANOTHER TOPIC LIKE THE WEATHER OR THE PRICE OF CAULIFLOWERS BUT IT WAS NO GOOD. LADY PRESCOTT WAS GETTING CARRIED AWAY AND THERE WAS JUST NO STOPPING HER NOW.

Birmingham 20 miles

SHE WAS LIKE A DRAGON BREATHING FIRE.

Sir Gerald's nickname is Niagara because he keeps bursting into tears. When I first met him he was a tiger but he's turned into a kitten. He's a stubborn, ignorant jelly and he drives me up the wall.

FREDERICK SAT IN A STATE OF SHOCK TRYING TO SQUEEZE WORDS THROUGH HIS FROZEN LIPS. BUT IT WAS JUST NO GOOD. HIS MOUTH OPENED AND CLOSED LIKE A DEMENTED GOLDFISH.

AND ALTHOUGH HE DID MANAGE A FEW INCOHERENT GRUNTS NONE OF THE SOUNDS CAME OUT RIGHT.

SO - RECOGNISING DEFEAT - HE GAVE UP TRYING TO CHANGE THE SUBJECT, SAT BACK AND JUST WATCHED THE VOLCANO ERUPT.

FREDERICK'S MIND WAS NOT AT PEACE. HERE HE WAS SITTING IN A ROLLS ROYCE DRIVEN BY THE WIFE OF THE GOVERNOR OF THE PRISON HE'D JUST ESCAPED FROM.

HE WAS MUMBLING, HIS STOMACH WAS RUMBLING, HIS CONFIDENCE WAS CRUMBLING, AND LADY PRESCOTT WAS GRUMBLING.

THE DRIVER PUT HER FOOT DOWN AND THE BLUE ROLLS ROYCE ROARED ON.

Perhaps I should have stayed in my cell.

Practice

12

kitten	sounds	wall	subject	name
volcano	Rolls Royce	prison	reputation	spine

1 Now that _____ rings a bell. I'm sure I've come across it somewhere before.

2 A cold shiver ran down his _____.

3 I know of him. He has quite a _____ in my field.

4 When I first met him, he was a tiger, but he's turned into a _____.

5 He drives me up the _____.

6 None of the _____ came out right.

7 So – recognising defeat – he gave up trying to change the _____,

8 ...sat back and just watched the _____ erupt.

9 Here he was sitting in a _____

10 ...driven by the wife of the governor of the _____ he'd just escaped from.

13

in	through	out	up	on
back	for	across	to	of

1 I'm very grateful _____ you, Mr... er...

2 Now that name rings a bell. I'm sure I've come _____ it somewhere before.

3 I know _____ him. He has quite a reputation in my field.

4 I'm sure it's a reputation _____ childish, incompetent stupidity!

5 Frederick sat _____ a state of shock,

6 ...trying to squeeze words _____ his frozen lips.

7 None of the sounds came _____ right.

8 So – recognising defeat – he gave _____ trying to change the subject,

9 ...sat _____ and just watched the volcano erupt.

10 The driver put her foot down and the blue Rolls Royce roared _____.

Notes

1 *on* often means 'to continue'.

'The blue Rolls Royce sped on down the M1.' (Chapter Seven)

'The driver put her foot down and the blue Rolls Royce roared on.' (Chapter Seven)

'He kept on proposing and I kept on saying "no".' (Chapter Nine)

'"Go on," Lady Prescott said gently.' (Chapter Ten)

'Karen Blackstone carried on talking, ignoring that last remark.' (Chapter Thirteen)

2 'That name rings a bell' = I've heard that name before

3 *to come across (something)* = to come into contact with (something)
unexpectedly or by chance

4 *Well I never!* = That's incredible! What a surprise!

5 'Perhaps you've heard of him' = Perhaps his name is familiar to you

6 'I know of him' = I've heard of him

7 A *grunt* (the noun) and *to grunt* (the verb) can also describe the sounds made by a pig and a tennis player.

8 *to give up* (= to stop or to abandon) can be used with a gerund or a noun.

'So – recognising defeat – he gave up trying to change the subject, sat back and just watched the volcano erupt.' (Chapter Seven)

'Frederick had given up trying to work out what was going on.' (Chapter Thirteen)

'I knew that I couldn't give Gerald up.' (Chapter Eight)

9 A few years ago, it was considered 'bad style' to put a preposition at the end of a sentence. Grammar books would tell you that 'To whom did you send the letter?' was better than 'Who did you send the letter to?'

But fashions and conventions change and these days it is quite acceptable to end a sentence with a preposition...

'Here he was, sitting in a Rolls Royce driven by the wife of the governor of the prison he'd just escaped from.' (Chapter Seven)

'I knew that I couldn't give Gerald up.' (Chapter Eight)

'I needed more time to think things through.' (Chapter Nine)

'...I suppose I needed someone to talk to.' (Chapter Ten)

'I can't let the children down.' (Chapter Eleven)

'They might even have let you off.' (Chapter Twelve)

'But where shall I send the papers to?' (Chapter Thirteen)

etc...

CHAPTER EIGHT

BY THE TIME THEY ARRIVED AT THE OUTSKIRTS OF BIRMINGHAM LADY PRESCOTT HAD CALMED DOWN A LITTLE AND FREDERICK WAS FEELING A BIT MORE RELAXED.

AND AS WE PICK UP THE STORY AGAIN (AT 1.23 P.M.) OUR TWO CHARACTERS HAVE STARTED TO GET ON SURPRISINGLY WELL...

THE BLUE ROLLS ROYCE SLOWED DOWN AND THEY DREW UP IN FRONT OF A ROW OF SHABBY TERRACED HOUSES.

Do you see number 42, the one with the pale green door? I was born there. And this little run down street on the edge of the city is where I grew up.

Whenever I feel down I come back here. This will always be my home. It's dirty and messy and some of the shops are boarded up. But as far as I'm concerned this is the best place in the world.

LADY PRESCOTT PUT ON THE HANDBRAKE, TOOK OFF HER SEATBELT AND STEPPED OUT OF THE CAR.

And now, Mr Carruthers, I'm going for a walk. Would you like me to show you around?

That would be very kind of you. But I don't want to put you to any trouble.

It would be no trouble at all. In fact you'd be doing me a favour. I've got a lot of things on my mind at the moment and I need someone to talk to. So I'd be very grateful if you came and walked with me.

LADY PRESCOTT LOCKED THE CAR.

THEY SET OFF ACROSS THE MARKET SQUARE ON A TOUR OF THE TOWN.

THEY CAME OVER THE NARROW STONE BRIDGE THAT CROSSED THE CANAL.

Has it changed much over the years?

No not really. They've done up some of the houses ... like these ones here ... but most of the properties are falling down or falling apart.

And - anyway - I'd be a bit sad if they knocked everything down and put up one of those ugly tower blocks. Perhaps it's better to keep it the way it is. I don't want them tearing down my childhood. They should leave my home alone.

You say this is your home. But then why did you go away?

Whenever there's an election, the politicians come round and knock on the door. They promise to pull down the terraced housing and build some new flats. But after the votes are counted, they never seem to get round to it. It's strange that, isn't it?

The story continues...

'Oh, that's simple,' Lady Prescott replied. 'I fell in love. Strange though it may seem, I left Birmingham to be with Gerald Prescott – the gutless, brainless, spineless fool who is now governor of Newtown Prison. You look a bit surprised, Mr Carruthers. Then perhaps I should explain.

There was a time when my husband was a bright, tender young man. It's only recently that he's turned into a workaholic who eats, drinks and sleeps prison life.

I met him when I was just eighteen. I was in my last term at school and Gerald was studying at the local technical college. He was absolutely broke and so he'd taken a part-time job at a take-away restaurant called The Birmingham Big Burger Bar. The take-away was in Crawford Street. It was on my way home from school. One day, I went in to get some chips. Gerald was serving behind the counter. He smiled at me and I felt a cold shiver run down my spine.

After that I went to the take-away every day. I wasn't hungry. I just wanted to see Gerald. Anyway, one afternoon he asked me out and we went for a walk in the park. We got on really well and I started seeing him all the time. He used to walk me to school in the morning and he'd come and pick me up when the classes were over. And then – all of a sudden – I fell in love with him. I don't know why. It just happened that way.

When my father found out what was going on, he went crazy. He didn't want his only daughter going out with someone who cooked hamburgers in a take-away. He told me that I had to stop seeing Gerald straightaway.

I had to make a choice. Should I obey my father and split up with the person I loved? Or should I defy my parents and go on seeing him? It didn't take me long to make up my mind! I knew that I couldn't give Gerald up. And so I had to work out some way of deceiving my parents.

The plan was simple. I pretended that I'd obeyed my father. I said that I'd broken up with Gerald. I cried for two or three days and went through ten packets of tissues. I stopped eating and slammed lots of doors. I put on a really good show. My parents were completely taken in.

But whenever my father's back was turned, I would slip out of the house and go and meet Gerald secretly, in the park or at the take-away. When I came home, I made up some story or other to explain where I'd been. "I was at a friend's house playing records" or "I was visiting a museum in the centre of the town".

My father seemed happy that I'd suddenly made lots of new friends who had money in their pockets and didn't cook burgers. But he didn't know what I was really up to...'

Lady Prescott suddenly broke off and – for the next minute or so – they walked on in silence. Frederick looked straight ahead. He said nothing. There was no need to talk. They crossed a main road and walked past a school. And then, as they turned down a narrow side street, Lady Prescott picked up the story again...

Practice

14

love	childhood	houses	spine	street
handbrake	seat belt	mind	workaholic	Gerald

1 This little run-down _____ on the edge of the city is where I grew up.

2 Lady Prescott put on the _____

3 ...and took off her _____.

4 They've done up some of the _____.

5 I don't want them tearing down my _____.

6 There was a time when my husband was a bright, tender young man. It's only recently that he's turned into a _____.

7 I felt a cold shiver run down my _____.

8 And then – all of a sudden – I fell in _____ with him.

9 It didn't take me long to make up my _____!

10 I knew that I couldn't give _____ up.

15

out	out	out	on	on
up	up	around	round	at

1 By the time they arrived _____ the outskirts of Birmingham, Lady Prescott had calmed down a little.

2 And as we pick up the story again, our two characters have started to get _____ surprisingly well.

3 This little run-down street on the edge of the city is where I grew _____.

4 And now, Mr Carruthers, I'm going for a walk. Would you like me to show you _____?

5 They've done _____ some of the houses...like these ones here...but most of the properties are falling down or falling apart.

6 But after the votes are counted, they never seem to get _____ to it. It's strange that, isn't it?

7 One afternoon, he asked me _____ and we went for a walk in the park.

8 When my father found _____ what

9 ...was going _____, he went crazy.

10 He didn't want his only daughter going _____ with someone who cooked hamburgers in a take-away.

Notes

1 *to calm down* = to relax

'By the time they arrived at the outskirts of Birmingham, Lady Prescott had calmed down a little...' (Chapter Eight)

'Now calm down. And go through the whole story right from the start.' (Chapter Two)

2 *to get on with (someone)* = to have a good relationship with (someone)

'...our two characters have started to get on surprisingly well.' (Chapter Eight)

'We got on really well and I started seeing him all the time.' (Chapter Eight)

3 *to feel down* = to feel depressed

'Whenever I feel down, I come back here.' (Chapter Eight)

'Frederick was staring deep into his coffee. Telling the story of the kidney machines had brought back some painful memories. And he suddenly felt very down.' (Chapter Twelve)

4 *to have something on your mind* = to be worried about something

'Lady Prescott paused. There was something on her mind.' (Chapter Ten)

'I've got a lot of things on my mind at the moment and I need someone to talk to.' (Chapter Eight)

5 Compare...

'And now, Mr Carruthers, I'm going for a walk. Would you like me to show you around?' (Chapter Eight)

and

'The woman showed them into the Managing Director's office and sniffed again.' (Chapter Twelve)

6 *to do up* (a flat, house, building, etc.) = to renovate, to repaint, to redecorate, etc.

'They've done up some of the houses...like these ones here...but most of the properties are falling down or falling apart.' (Chapter Eight)

◆ They did up the flat and then sold it.

7 *to come round (here)* = to go round (there) = to visit

'The politicians come round and knock on the door.' (Chapter Eight)

'Gerald went round to see my father. They had a long talk and – somehow – they sorted the whole thing out.' (Chapter Nine)

8 *to get round to* (= to find the time to do something) is often used in a slightly negative sense, suggesting that someone is too lazy, too uncaring or too selfish to bother to do something...

'But after the votes are counted, they never seem to get round to it. It's strange that, isn't it?' (Chapter Eight)

(Lady Prescott is suggesting that once the politicians are elected, they no longer care about the people who voted for them.)

9 *going on* = happening

'When my father found out what was going on, he went crazy.' (Chapter Eight)

'He'd realised what had been going on behind his back.' (Chapter Nine)

CHAPTER NINE

On my last day at school Gerald asked me to marry him. As you can imagine I felt tremendously flattered. But I turned him down. I told him I was just too young to settle down. I needed more time to think things through.

For the next few months we played a sort of game. He kept on proposing and I kept on saying 'No'.

But then one night — it was May 10th — everything changed. I told my father I was going to a poetry reading in the local Town Hall. In fact, I slipped out of the side door and went to the cinema with Gerald.

When the film was over we caught the last bus home but — along the way — the bus broke down and all the passengers had to get off and walk.

It was four miles from the city centre to my house and by the time we got home it was very late. Gerald saw me to the door, kissed me on the cheek and then said goodnight.

It was now 2 o'clock in the morning. I took out my key and let myself in as quietly as I could. My father was waiting for me in the hall. He normally went to bed at about 11 but — that night — he'd decided to stay up until I got in.

He was furious. He'd seen Gerald bringing me to the door and — at that moment — he'd realised what had been going on behind his back. I'd never seen my father so angry. I thought he was going to hit me! So, I ran past him and went straight up to bed!

The next morning at breakfast we had a huge row. He shouted at me. I shouted at him. And it ended up with me packing a suitcase and storming out of the house. I went straight round to Gerald's flat and we decided to run away.

Can you imagine it? Me and Gerald running away!

Anyway, to cut a long story short, we eloped to Newtown and got married in the local church. It was a very quiet wedding. Just me, Gerald, the vicar and a couple of witnesses. All very romantic!

As soon as the service was over I rang up my parents to tell them what we'd done.

My father was stunned and hurt. He lost his temper and slammed down the phone.

For the next few months we went through a really bad patch. I didn't go back to the house and whenever I rang home there were long pregnant pauses. It was all very awkward.

But then one day Gerald went round to see my father. They had a long talk and — somehow — they sorted the whole thing out. I made it up with my parents and since then we've been very close.

And I suppose that now — looking back — I can appreciate what my mother and father were going through. I was their only daughter and they didn't think my husband was good enough for me.

After all, when Gerald was younger he wasn't exactly rolling in money. He was so hard up that he'd use the same tea bag for a week. He owned three socks and they all had holes in them. His shirt sleeves were frayed and his trousers were held up with string.

LADY PRESCOTT SIGHED AND SMILED. A SINGLE TEAR RAN DOWN HER CHEEK.

Ah, those were happy days.

The story continues...

Lady Prescott broke off and – once again – they walked on in silence.

It was now mid-afternoon and the streets were empty. There was a stillness in the cool summer air, as if the world had paused for thought. No birds sang. No cows mooed. No ducks quacked. No sheep baaed. No dogs woofed. No cats miaowed. In fact, on that bright, soft, tranquil day, there was only one sound to be heard – the low, continuous rumbling of Frederick's empty stomach, for twenty-four hours starved of food.

They walked down a couple of alleyways and then, as they turned into the main road, they came upon a postman riding a bicycle. The bicycle was very old and it had no springs. And so, as he rode across the cobblestones, he seemed to be nodding his head and shaking his head all at the same time.

Lady Prescott was talking again: 'Do you know where we are, Mr Carruthers? This is Crawford Street. And at the end of this row of shops, there's The Birmingham Big Burger Bar – where I met Gerald all those years ago. Look, I don't know about you, but I'm starving. Why don't we pop in there and have a late lunch? They serve the best beefburgers in town!'

Frederick seemed a little agitated. 'I could do with a meal too,' he said. 'But I'm afraid I don't have a penny on me. You see, I went out in rather a hurry last night.'

Lady Prescott smiled. 'But you must be my guest, Mr Carruthers. You've gone out of your way to help me and you've put up with all my complaints about Sir Gerald. Paying for lunch will be my way of paying you back for all your kindness. Come on, I insist. I've had a long and difficult day. I'm tired out and very worked up about my husband. I need a good meal to calm me down and I don't want to eat alone.'

Practice

16

penny	cheek	key	proposing	husband
way	complaints	phone	money	back

1 He kept on _____ and I kept on saying 'no'.

2 I took out my _____ and let myself in.

3 At that moment, he'd realised what had been going on behind

his _____.

4 He lost his temper and slammed down the _____.

5 When Gerald was younger, he wasn't exactly rolling in _____.

6 Lady Prescott sighed and smiled. A single tear ran down her

_____.

7 I'm afraid I don't have a _____ on me.

8 You've gone out of your _____ to help me.

9 You've put up with all my _____ about Sir Gerald.

10 I'm tired out and very worked up about my _____.

17	out	out	to	to	with
	on	on	through	at	at

1 On my last day _____ school, Gerald asked me to marry him.

2 I needed more time to think things _____.

3 He kept _____ proposing.

4 I told my father I was going _____ a poetry reading in the local Town Hall.

5 I took _____ my key and let myself in.

6 He'd realised what had been going _____ behind his back.

7 He shouted _____ me.

8 We eloped _____ Newtown and got married in the local church.

9 They had a long talk and – somehow – they sorted the whole thing _____.

10 You've put up _____ all my complaints about Sir Gerald.

Notes

1 *to turn (someone or something) down* = to say 'no' to (an offer, proposal, suggestion or application)

2 *to settle down* can mean 'to start to live in one place or situation permanently'.

  'I was just too young to settle down.' (Chapter Nine)

But notice a slightly different meaning in Chapter Fifteen:

  'The prisoners had settled down for the night and the jail was locked and still.'

3 *to think (something) through* = to think (something) over
= to consider (a proposal, plan, situation, etc.) very carefully

  'I needed more time to think things through.' (Chapter Nine)

  '"We're going to give you twenty-four hours to think it over," he said.' (Chapter Eleven)

4 'I let myself in' = I opened the door with a key

5 *it ended up...* = the result was...

6 *a pregnant pause* = an embarrassing silence

7 *to sort (something) out* = to solve (a problem, issue, argument, dispute, etc.)

  'Gerald went round to see my father...and – somehow – they sorted the whole thing out.' (Chapter Nine)

  'We had a long talk on the phone and we sorted a few things out.' (Chapter Thirteen)

8 *to make it up with (someone)* = to re-establish a friendship or a loving relationship

9 *rolling in money* = very rich

10 *hard up* = very poor

LADY PRESCOTT WAS RIGHT ABOUT THE FOOD. IT WAS DEFINITELY THE BEST BURGER THAT FREDERICK HAD EVER TASTED. BUT THAT WAS HARDLY SURPRISING. HE WAS SO HUNGRY THAT HE COULD HAVE EATEN THE SERVIETTES AND THE CHEAP BLUE PLASTIC TRAY.

It's 3 o'clock. I've been rabbiting on about my problems for over an hour now. Look, I'm sorry. I didn't mean to burden you. It's just that after my bust-up with Sir Gerald I suppose I needed someone to talk to.

Mr. Carruthers, I want to ask you a question. When I drove into that layby you were standing around with your hands in your pockets looking like a down-and-out.

LADY PRESCOTT PAUSED. THERE WAS SOMETHING ON HER MIND.

But you have an honest, kindly face and you're obviously an intelligent man. So how did you end up like that?

There must be something wrong. And I think it's time for you to tell me the truth. Why were you wandering around near the motorway with no money in your pocket and those very strange clothes?

FREDERICK SAID NOTHING. HE LOOKED DOWN AT THE TABLE AND STIRRED HIS COFFEE WITH A SPOON. HE DIDN'T KNOW WHAT TO DO. HE WANTED TO EXPLAIN THINGS BUT HE WASN'T SURE WHETHER HE COULD TRUST LADY PRESCOTT. AFTER ALL, SHE WAS THE WIFE OF THE GOVERNOR OF THE PRISON HE'D JUST ESCAPED FROM. IF SHE FOUND OUT THAT HE WAS A CONVICT ON THE RUN PERHAPS SHE'D TURN HIM IN AND THEN HE MIGHT END UP IN CELL 269 AGAIN.

FREDERICK LOOKED UP. HE BROKE THE SILENCE.

You're right of course. It is strange that I should be drifting around with nowhere to go. And yes I am in trouble. But if I told you what I've gone through in the past few months you might get angry. And that would make things worse.

LADY PRESCOTT FINISHED OFF HER FRENCH FRIES AND SMILED.

You've no reason to be afraid. If you're in trouble then you need help. And if there's something on your mind you shouldn't just bottle it up inside you. You should tell me about it and get it off your chest. Then you'd feel a lot better. And I give you my word that I won't get angry, whatever you say.

Sugar

The story continues...

Frederick sighed. 'Perhaps you're right,' he said. 'And, after all, what have I got to lose? Well, the truth is that up until two years ago, I was leading a very simple and predictable life. I had a steady job, a beautiful home and a loving family. Then, all of a sudden, something happened that changed everything. My whole world just fell apart.'

Frederick broke off. He seemed a little uneasy.

'Go on,' Lady Prescott said gently.

'Well, it's a very long story,' Frederick replied. 'And I don't really know where to begin.'

'Try the beginning,' said Lady Prescott, putting a straw into her milkshake. 'I'm in no hurry. I'm going to drink this very, very slowly.'

Frederick took a deep breath and picked up the story again. 'My mother is a nurse in a small hospital,' he said. 'She looks after sick children. She's a wonderful, extraordinary woman and she works incredibly hard.

One day, I drove down to the hospital to pick my mother up after work. We were going out to dinner. I parked the car and, as I was walking through one of the wards, I could hear a child crying very softly. I looked across and saw a little boy. He must have been about eight or nine. He was so ill that he couldn't sit up in bed properly. He had to lie against pillows all day long. It was terrible. He was pale, lifeless, too weak to move.

The next day, I rang up the manager of the hospital and asked about the little boy. She told me that all the children in that ward had problems with their kidneys.

"And is there nothing you can do?" I asked.

"I'm afraid not," she said. "What we really need is half a dozen kidney machines. Then the children would be able to get out of bed and walk around the ward. But, unfortunately, the hospital is very short of money. We're so hard up that we can't afford to buy one machine, let alone six. So, I'm afraid the children will just have to suffer."

When I put down the phone, I felt terribly disturbed. It was so sad, so shocking, so unfair. I decided that I had to find a way to help the children. I couldn't stand by and do nothing.

At first, I couldn't think what to do. But then – all of a sudden – I came up with an idea. I was a bank manager and a lot of money passed through my hands. During a normal working day, I would write out ten, maybe twelve, official cheques for different things – stationery, coffee, furniture, stamps and so on. I'd worked at the bank for thirty years, so everybody knew me. And nobody ever checked up on what I was doing. I suppose I had an honest face and they just trusted me!

One afternoon – it was a Wednesday – I called my secretary into the office and told her to cancel my appointments. When she'd left the room, I took the phone off the hook and drew the curtains. Then I took the official cheque book out of the safe and wrote a cheque to myself!

    Pay Mr F. Carruthers,
    £100.00 only
    Signed Frederick Carruthers.

It was breathtakingly, outrageously simple. A bank manager stealing money from his own bank!'

Practice

18 Revision Exercise

In Chapters Five to Ten, who...

	FREDERICK	LADY PRESCOTT	SIR GERALD	LADY PRESCOTT'S FATHER
1 ...held out his hand?				
2 ...felt a bit let down?				
3 ...took off the handbrake?				
4 ...was like a dragon breathing fire?				
5 ...sat back?				
6 ...put her foot down?				
7 ...calmed down?				
8 ...grew up at number 42?				
9 ...showed Frederick around?				
10 ...had a lot of things on her mind?				
11 ...worked in a take-away?				
12 ...kept on proposing?				
13 ...kept on saying 'no'?				
14 ...took out a key?				
15 ...stayed up?				
16 ...stormed out of the house?				
17 ...eloped to Newtown?				
18 ...slammed down the phone?				
19 ...rabbited on?				
20 ...came up with an idea?				

Notes

1 *to rabbit on* = to talk on and on and on and on...

2 a *bust-up* = an argument

3 *to bottle (something) up inside you* is the opposite of 'to get (something) off your chest'.

4 Compare...

'My whole world just fell apart.' (Chapter Ten)

'But most of the properties are falling down or falling apart.' (Chapter Eight)

and

'How could a good man end up like this? He's falling apart.' (Chapter Twelve)

5 *to break off* = to pause; to stop talking

6 *out* often means 'outside the house'.

'Anyway, one afternoon, he asked me out and we went for a walk in the park.' (Chapter Eight)

'We were going out to dinner.' (Chapter Ten)

'And that night, the Carruthers family, Angus Macpherson and Sir Gerald and Lady Prescott dined out in style.' (Chapter Fourteen)

Chapter eleven

At the age of 45 I was about to commit my first crime. I looked at the cheque. My head was spinning. This was robbery. Was I doing the right thing? Could I get away with it? Should I just tear up the cheque and throw it away? Perhaps I should forget about the whole thing.

But then I thought about the children in the hospital. They needed the money more than the bank. I was stealing it for them.

So, I took a deep breath, folded the cheque up and put it into my pocket.

I left the office and took a taxi to another branch of the bank. I knew one of the cashiers there. We chatted for a while. And then, with my heart pounding, I paid the cheque into my current account. Three days later the payment cleared. I had stolen my first £100.
The following week I did the whole thing again. Another cheque. The same branch. The same cashier. The same fear. The same excitement when the money was cleared into my account.

And so it went on. Week after week I stole money from the bank and each cheque was a little bigger than the last.

You've no idea how I felt. I was risking everything I had – my career, my family life, my reputation. But, nothing was going to stop me now. The image of the little boy crying on his pillow haunted me. I couldn't get it out of my mind. And I had to do something to help.

I think the next few weeks were the most exciting of my life. In some strange way I'd suddenly come alive. I was sharp, human, burning with anger. And I suppose I got a bit carried away.
I was soon writing cheques for five and ten thousand pounds. It was crazy. Sometimes, the cashier seemed a bit suspicious. She couldn't work out what the payments were for. But – each week – I made up some new story to explain the cheques away. And she fell for it every time.

I suppose it never occurred to her that Frederick Carruthers - her punctual, conscientious friend - could have turned into a common thief, an embezzler, a liar, a man obsessed.

By that summer I'd managed to save up a quarter of a million pounds.

One morning I didn't go into work. I walked into the hospital and wrote out a cheque for every penny I had. The manager went straight out and bought six new kidney machines.

A few days later we had a small ceremony in the ward. It was a bit like launching a ship, or opening a bridge! I unwrapped the machines, plugged them in and switched them on. And then as the lights flashed the children gave me a round of applause that seemed to go on forever. I felt very proud. It was the best moment of my life.

The story continues...

But then – inevitably, I suppose – my luck failed.

Someone at Head Office became suspicious. How could a branch manager afford to donate £250,000 to a hospital?

The Head of Finance went to the central computer and started going through my account. She noticed that I'd been building up large amounts of cash. But how could I save up so much money on the salary I earned? She smelt a rat and, when she looked into the strange dealings on the branch account, she knew that something was wrong.

Anyway, it wasn't long before she'd put two and two together and worked out what I'd been up to. She tipped off the police and, when I turned up for work the next morning, there were three detectives waiting in my office. They took me down to the police station and that was it. I was charged with theft and my world just fell apart. The trial was fixed for December 18th – just one week before Christmas!

Two days before I was due in court, a director of the bank came to see me. He came straight to the point. He offered me a deal. He said they would drop all the charges if I paid the money back.

"But how can I do that?" I asked. "The hospital have spent it all."

"That's simple," the man said. "Tell the hospital that you've changed your mind. Tell them it was all a mistake. Just tell them to send the machines back."

"But what about the children?" I said.

The man shrugged his shoulders. "Our bank is a business, Mr Carruthers. It's not a charity. And if you don't get our money back, you'll end up in jail. It's as simple as that. It's up to you. But you can't have it both ways."

He stood up. "We're going to give you twenty-four hours to think it over," he said. "You don't have to decide right away. You can sleep on it. I'll come back tomorrow and you can tell me what you've decided. But just remember one thing, Mr Carruthers. You can't rip the bank off and expect to get away with it. Life's not like that. And we will hunt you down until we get every penny of our money back. I trust I've made myself clear. Good afternoon."

That night, I lay awake in my cell and thought the whole thing through. Was I being stupid? Should I save my own skin? Was it all worth fighting for? I went over it again and again.

The man from the bank came back the next day. He walked into my cell with a stupid smirk on his face. He was so sure of himself. So confident. He thought I was going to give in without a fight. He sat down and grinned at me. And at that moment, I noticed he had false teeth.

"So, Mr Carruthers," he began. "I trust that you've come to your senses. I've prepared this letter for you to sign. It instructs the hospital to send the items in question back to the factory and..."

I held up my hand and the man from the bank stopped talking.

"You can save your breath," I said. "Put the letter away. I've got no intention of signing it. I've decided to go through with the trial. I can't let the children down. I promised them six kidney machines and I'm not going back on my word."

The man from the bank gaped at me and his false teeth fell out. They crashed noisily onto the floor and rolled under my bed. I bent down, picked them up and handed them back to him.

"I believe these are yours," I said. You should have seen his face!

And so the trial went ahead. I pleaded guilty, the judge sentenced me to three years in jail and that's how I ended up in...' Frederick paused and took a deep breath,'...in Newtown Prison...from where I escaped at eleven o'clock last night.'

Lady Prescott blinked twice. She didn't seem at all shocked or upset by the fact that Frederick was a convict on the run from her husband's jail. In fact, her one and only concern was for the children in the ward.

Practice

19

account	hand	jail	story	cheque
payments	trial	police	bank	office

1 I looked at the _____ . My head was spinning.

2 She couldn't work out what the _____ were for.

3 But – each week – I made up some new _____ to explain the cheques away.

4 The Head of Finance went to the central computer and started going through my _____ .

5 She tipped off the _____

6 ...and when I turned up for work the next morning, there were three detectives waiting in my _____.

7 If you don't get our money back, you'll end up in _____.

8 You can't rip the _____ off and expect to get away with it.

9 I held up my _____ and the man from the bank stopped talking.

10 I've decided to go through with the _____.

20

through	in	in	to	with
up	of	of	for	for

1 It's up _____ you.

2 That night, I lay awake _____ my cell

3 ...and thought the whole thing _____.

4 Was it all worth fighting _____?

5 He was so sure _____ himself.

6 He thought I was going to give _____ without a fight.

7 I've prepared this letter _____ you to sign.

8 I've got no intention _____ signing it.

9 I've decided to go through _____ the trial.

10 And that's how I ended _____ in Newtown Prison.

Notes

1 'It was a bit like launching a ship...' (Chapter Eleven)
You can also launch a rocket, a campaign, a new product and an attack.

2 'she smelt a rat' = she became suspicious; she realised that something
was wrong

3 *to be up to (something)* = to be acting secretly, suspiciously or
conspiratorially

4 Compare...

'...a director of the bank came to see me.' (Chapter Eleven)

'He came straight to the point.' (Chapter Eleven)

and

'I trust that you've come to your senses.' (Chapter Eleven)

You can also come to an agreement and to a conclusion.

5 'It's up to you' = It's your decision

6 *to rip (someone) off* = to cheat (someone); to trick (someone); to take unfair
advantage of (someone)

'You can't rip the bank off and expect to get away with it.' (Chapter Eleven)

'And Karen Blackstone got a promise that the Head of Charity Donations
would never let on how to rip off the bank.' (Chapter Thirteen)

7 *to give in* = to surrender; to stop fighting

CHAPTER TWELVE

There's one thing I don't understand. Why didn't you tell the court what you did with the money? Then they would have seen things in a different light. They would have reduced your sentence. They might even have let you off.

I thought of that. But then the judge would have ordered the hospital to sell the machines and pay the money back. And that was the last thing I wanted. I may have got out of going to prison but what would have happened to the children? I couldn't take that risk.

LADY PRESCOTT SHOOK HER HEAD.

I can't decide if you were very brave or very stupid. But I have to admire what you did. And you nearly got away with it. You were really quite unlucky.

Now I don't condone stealing. Theft is theft and you deserved to be punished. But after two years in jail you've paid off your debt.

A SILENCE FELL BETWEEN THEM. FREDERICK WAS STARING DEEP INTO HIS COFFEE. TELLING THE STORY OF THE KIDNEY MACHINES HAD BROUGHT BACK SOME PAINFUL MEMORIES. AND HE SUDDENLY FELT VERY DOWN.

How could a good man end up like this? He's falling apart. I must help him. I can't just stand by and do nothing.

AND WITH THAT SHE SUDDENLY STOOD UP AND PICKED UP HER BAG.

Would you excuse me, Mr Carruthers? I have a couple of calls to make.

LADY PRESCOTT WALKED OVER TO THE PAY PHONE IN THE CORNER OF THE ROOM. SHE TOOK A YELLOW DIARY OUT OF THE BAG AND LOOKED UP A NUMBER. THEN SHE PICKED UP THE RECEIVER, PUT SOME COINS INTO THE SLOT AND STARTED DIALLING.

FREDERICK TURNED HIS FACE AND LOOKED OUT AT CRAWFORD STREET. THERE WERE NOW LOTS OF PEOPLE ABOUT. IT WAS HALF PAST THREE AND THE LOCAL SCHOOL HAD JUST BROKEN UP FOR THE DAY. A YOUNG GIRL CAME IN AND ORDERED SOME CHIPS.

LADY PRESCOTT FINISHED HER FIRST CALL AND PUT DOWN THE PHONE. THEN SHE TURNED ROUND AND LOOKED ACROSS AT FREDERICK. HE WAS MILES AWAY, STARING OUT OF THE WINDOW.

SHE PICKED UP THE PHONE AGAIN AND DIALLED A SECOND NUMBER.

A FEW MINUTES LATER SHE WAS THROUGH.

Is that Newtown Prison? This is Lady Prescott. I want to speak to my husband.

The story continues...

Lady Prescott came back to the table and sat down. 'I made a call to a friend of mine, Mr Carruthers. She'd like to meet you. I said we'd be in her office just after five. So why don't you drink up your coffee and eat up your cheeseburger and finish off the French fries, and then we can set off.'

'But where are we going?' Frederick said. 'And who is your friend?'

'For the moment, that must remain a secret,' Lady Prescott replied. 'But she's an important woman and I think she can help you. Oh, and do cheer up, Mr Carruthers. You mustn't worry so much. It'll all work out in the end.'

Frederick drank up his coffee, ate up his cheeseburger, finished off his French fries and then stood up.

They walked back to the car – along Crawford Street, down a couple of side alleys, over the stone bridge that crossed the canal. And a few minutes later, the blue Rolls Royce was on the road again.

Frederick was exhausted. The last twenty-four hours were beginning to catch up with him. And, as the car sped on down the motorway, he closed his eyes and gently nodded off, falling ever deeper into sleep.

◆ ◆ ◆ ◆ ◆ ◆ ◆ ◆ ◆

A couple of hours later, Frederick felt someone tapping on his shoulder. 'Come along, Mr Carruthers,' Lady Prescott said. 'Wake up. We're nearly there.'

Frederick woke up with a start. And at first he thought he was still dreaming. Because there – right ahead of them – was a vast glass and metal building that he knew all too well. But this was no dream. And their car was heading straight for the main entrance.

'Where are you taking me?' Frederick shouted. 'This is the Head Office of my old bank. You've set me up, haven't you? You're going to turn me in! I should never have trusted you. Stop the car right now! Let me out!'

Frederick took off his seat belt and tried to get out of the car. But Lady Prescott turned round and dragged him back inside.

'For goodness' sake, calm down, Mr Carruthers,' she said. 'I haven't set you up and I'm not going to turn you in. And don't get so worked up. You're as bad as my husband. Now just listen to me. When we were in the take-away, I rang up your Head Office and fixed up an appointment with Karen Blackstone. She's a good friend of mine. We went to school together.'

'Karen Blackstone?' Frederick said. 'But she's the Managing Director of the bank.'

'Exactly, Mr Carruthers. And we're on our way to her office. She's going to give you a new job.'

'You must be joking,' said Frederick. 'The bank would never dream of taking me on again. I've got a criminal record for stealing their money.'

'Well, just you wait and see,' Lady Prescott replied. 'I think you're in for a surprise.'

The blue Rolls Royce pulled up in front of a huge skyscraper that seemed to pierce the clouds. They got out of the car and walked through into the main lobby. Then they made their way to the Managing Director's penthouse suite. As the lift rose smoothly to the eighty-ninth floor, Frederick broke out into a cold sweat.

A thousand thoughts were running through his mind. Could he really trust Lady Prescott? Was he walking into a trap? Would the police be there to arrest him again? And what would Karen Blackstone make of his clothes? He stared at himself in the mirror. He wasn't exactly dressed up for the occasion. In the past twenty-four hours, he'd crawled through mud, swum across lakes, climbed up trees, jumped onto trains, rolled down hills and put a spare wheel onto the blue Rolls Royce. And now, after all that, he looked like a scarecrow in a thunderstorm. The stains on his shirt and his crumpled prison trousers didn't quite fit in with the thick-pile carpet and the soft leather chairs.

When the lift doors opened, they were met by a tall, angular secretary who took one look at Frederick's bedraggled appearance and gave a shrill sniff of disapproval. The woman showed them into the Managing Director's office and sniffed again. Then she turned and closed the door behind her.

Practice

21

clothes	hours	people	prison	number
office	surprise	start	mind	diary

1 I may have got out of going to _____, but what would have happened to the children?

2 She took a yellow _____ out of the bag

3 ...and looked up a _____.

4 There were now lots of _____ about.

5 Frederick was exhausted. The last twenty-four _____ were beginning to catch up with him.

6 Frederick woke up with a _____.

7 I think you're in for a _____.

8 A thousand thoughts were running through his _____.

9 And what would Karen Blackstone make of his _____?

10 The woman showed them into the Managing Director's _____ and sniffed again.

22

of	of	off	up	up
out	to	with	apart	for

1 They would have reduced your sentence. They might even have let you _____.

2 I may have got out _____ going to prison, but what would have happened to the children?

3 You nearly got away _____ it. You were really quite unlucky.

4 How could a good man end up like this? He's falling _____.

5 This is the Head Office of the bank. You've set me _____, haven't you?

6 Stop the car right now! Let me _____!

7 And don't get so worked _____. You're as bad as my husband.

8 Now just listen _____ me.

9 I've got a criminal record _____ stealing their money.

10 And what would Karen Blackstone make _____ his clothes?

Notes

1 Note the use of...
  a *to let (someone) off*
  b *to get away with (something)*
  c *to get out of (doing something)*

These three phrasal verbs are used when talking about crime and punishment.

  a *to let (someone) off* = to choose not to punish (someone) for a mistake, sin, error or crime

'They would have reduced your sentence. They might even have let you off.' (Chapter Twelve)

  b *to get away with (something)* = not to be punished for a mistake, sin, error or crime

'But I have to admire what you did. And you nearly got away with it.' (Chapter Twelve)

  c *to get out of (doing something)* = to avoid doing something you dislike or fear

'I may have got out of going to prison, but what would have happened to the children?' (Chapter Twelve)

2 *to look up (something)* = to look (something) up
                  = to find information in a diary, timetable, reference book, etc.

'She took a yellow diary out of the bag and looked up a number.' (Chapter Twelve)

3 *he was miles away* = he was daydreaming; he wasn't concentrating

4 *Cheer up!* = Don't be so sad!

5 *to get worked up* = to become excited, anxious, tense, nervous, etc. (You can also say *to be worked up*.)

WITH THE INTRODUCTIONS OVER, KAREN BLACKSTONE SAT DOWN AND PICKED UP A PENCIL.

Right, let's get down to business. I've been going through your file, Mr Carruthers. As far as I can see you were a model employee — punctual, industrious, conscientious, loyal. Then came the incident with the kidney machines and you threw away thirty years of hard work.
But there are two things in your favour. You know the bank inside out and you're obviously committed to charity work. And that makes you just the person we're looking for.

What do you mean? I don't understand.

Then let me explain. Over the past few months the bank has run into some problems. For some reason we've been losing a lot of business.

It's a worrying trend. And so - last week - we carried out a survey to find out what's wrong. We discovered, Mr Carruthers, that the Bank is not universally loved.

It seems that because we don't sponsor operas or football teams or dog shows people think we're mean. The public sees us as selfish, ruthless and greedy. To put it bluntly, our image puts people off.

But this can't go on. And so something has to change. I want the Bank to come across in a more human, caring way. I want people to look on us as a friend, not as an enemy. I want people to come to us with their problems.

...and with their cash!

KAREN BLACKSTONE CARRIED ON TALKING, IGNORING THAT LAST REMARK.

Now when I heard the story of you and the kidney machines it set me thinking. We make a solid return on our capital. And it wouldn't do us any harm to give away some of those profits to worthy causes in the community.... hospitals, voluntary groups, youth clubs and so on.
Just think of it, Mr Carruthers. Just think of all the good we could do!

And just think of it, Mrs Blackstone. Just think of all that tax-deductible, cheap publicity.

THE MANAGING DIRECTOR SMILED AND THEN PICKED UP HER THEME AGAIN.

And this is where you come in Mr Carruthers. I'd like you to come back to the Bank and set the whole thing up. I'm offering you a new job — Head of Charity Donations.

CHARITY DEPARTME

The story continues...

'And if I was to take up this new challenge,' Frederick said, 'you'd expect me to keep quiet about the events of two years ago. You wouldn't want me to reveal how I showed up the flaws in your security system. In other words, you want to buy my silence.'

Karen Blackstone was drumming her pencil on the table. 'Let's be practical, Mr Carruthers. Not every convict can leave prison and walk straight back into a job. It's very simple. I need you and you need me. It's a case of you scratch my back, I'll scratch yours. I think we understand each other perfectly!'

And so a deal was struck. Frederick got a new job. And Karen Blackstone got a promise that the Head of Charity Donations would never let on how to rip off the bank.

'You'll have your new contract in the morning,' Karen Blackstone said. 'But where shall I send the papers to?'

The question hung in the air like a vulture. It suddenly dawned on Frederick that he couldn't take up a new job until he'd served out his term in jail. And he just didn't know what to say.

Lady Prescott leaned forward. 'If I could just butt in here,' she said. 'I think I've sorted out that problem, too. I made two phone calls from the take-away, Mr Carruthers. The first was to Karen, as you know. The second was to my husband. And you'll be leaving prison much sooner than you think.'

◆ ◆ ◆ ◆ ◆ ◆ ◆ ◆ ◆

It was now 5.35 and the blue Rolls Royce was coming home.

'Could you tell me what's going on?' Frederick said. 'I'm getting a bit confused.'

'Well, it's all quite simple,' Lady Prescott replied. 'I'm going back to my husband. We had a long talk on the phone and we sorted a few things out.'

'But where does that leave me?' Frederick asked. 'Are you going to turn me in?'

'Not exactly.' Lady Prescott smiled. 'I'm going to smuggle you back into the prison and then the governor's going to let you out.'

Frederick seemed a bit confused. 'I'm not with you,' he said.

Lady Prescott took a deep breath. 'Gerald tells me that you've served two thirds of your sentence. And since you've been a model prisoner, you're now due for parole. There was no need for you to run off like that. They were going to let you out anyway.'

Frederick was getting lost again.

'Let me put it another way,' Lady Prescott said. 'If you'd stayed in, instead of breaking out, the governor would have let you off the last twelve months of your sentence and let you out one year early!'

Frederick's eyebrows collided with each other. The demented goldfish had returned.

Lady Prescott pulled in and stopped the car. 'We'll be there in a few minutes,' she said. 'I've taken a blanket out of the boot. I think it's time for you to hide.'

Frederick had given up trying to work out what was going on. So, rather sulkily, he climbed over onto the back seat and covered himself up. A few moments later, the blue Rolls Royce moved off again and headed for Newtown.

By the time they arrived at the prison gates, night was falling. Lady Prescott slowed down and stopped the car. Then she wound down her window and leaned across.

Practice

23

profits	problem	friend	jail	job
image	survey	Frederick	file	pencil

1 Karen Blackstone sat down and picked up a _____ .

2 I've been going through your _____ , Mr Carruthers.

3 We carried out a _____ to find out what's wrong.

4 To put it bluntly, our _____ puts people off.

5 I want people to look on us as a _____ .

6 It wouldn't do us any harm to give away some of those _____ to worthy causes in the community.

7 It suddenly dawned on _____ that

8 ...he couldn't take up a new _____

9 ...until he'd served out his term in _____ .

10 I think I've sorted out that _____ , too.

24

out	out	out	out	as
off	to	up	through	on

1 I've been going _____ your file, Mr Carruthers.

2 We carried _____ a survey

3 ...to find _____ what's wrong.

4 The public sees us _____ selfish, ruthless and greedy.

5 To put it bluntly, our image puts people _____ .

6 But where shall I send the papers _____ ?

7 I think I've sorted _____ that problem, too.

8 Frederick had given _____

9 ...trying to work _____

10 ...what was going _____ .

Notes

1 *to go through* = to check

2 '...we carried out a survey...' (Chapter Thirteen)
You can also carry out an investigation, an attack and a threat.

3 'The public sees us as selfish, ruthless and greedy.' (Chapter Thirteen)
'I want people to look on us as a friend, not as an enemy.' (Chapter Thirteen)

Notice how...

to see (someone or something) as =

to look on (someone or something) as =

to consider (someone or something) to be

4 Notice how *to go on, to carry on* and *to keep on* are followed by a gerund...

'Karen Blackstone carried on talking, ignoring that last remark.' (Chapter Thirteen)

'He kept on proposing and I kept on saying "no".' (Chapter Nine)

'Or should I defy my parents and go on seeing him?' (Chapter Eight)

5 Compare...

to show up (something) = to reveal (something) that was previously hidden

'You wouldn't want me to reveal how I showed up the flaws in your security system.' (Chapter Thirteen)

and

to show (someone) up = to embarrass (someone) in public

6 *a flaw* = a weakness

Note also: 'a flawless diamond' and 'a flawless performance'.

7 *to let on* = to reveal (a secret)

'And Karen Blackstone got a promise that the Head of Charity Donations would never let on how to rip off the bank.' (Chapter Thirteen)

'But don't let on that you managed to break out.' (Chapter Fourteen)

8 *to butt in* = to interrupt

CHAPTER FOURTEEN

Good evening, Mr Thomas. And how are you tonight?

I'm fine thanks ma'am. We're very glad to see you again.

THE GUARD SALUTED, PRESSED A BUTTON AND WAVED THE CAR THROUGH.

HM PRISONS RULES

THE HUGE IRON GATES SWUNG OPEN AND LADY PRESCOTT DROVE THROUGH INTO THE MAIN PRISON SQUARE. THEN SHE TURNED DOWN A DIMLY-LIT ALLEY WHERE SHE SLOWED DOWN AND PARKED THE CAR.

SHE FLASHED HER HEADLIGHTS AND ANGUS - FOR SOME REASON WEARING A FALSE MOUSTACHE AND A PAIR OF DARK GLASSES - CAME OUT FROM BEHIND A LARGE GREY DUSTBIN AND WAVED.

LADY PRESCOTT GOT OUT OF THE CAR AND LOOKED AROUND. THERE WAS NO ONE ELSE ABOUT.

You can come out now Mr Carruthers. The coast is clear. And Mr Macpherson is waiting for you.

FREDERICK SLIPPED OUT OF THE CAR AND RAN DOWN THE ALLEY.

Welcome back Sir. I'm so glad to see you again. I thought I was going to lose my job when you disappeared. I shouldn't have nodded off you see. It was all my fault.

FREDERICK SMILED AND THEY SLIPPED THROUGH A SIDE GATE INTO THE MAIN WING OF THE PRISON.

ANGUS TOOK THE KEYS OFF HIS BELT AND UNLOCKED CELL 269. THEN HE PUSHED OPEN THE DOOR AND STEPPED BACK.

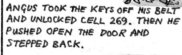

After you Mr Carruthers. After you.

FREDERICK WALKED INTO THE CELL AND SAT DOWN.

It feels so strange to be back here. Six hours ago I was in the Birmingham Big Burger Bar eating a cheeseburger and french fries. Three hours later I was in the Head Office of the bank. And now I'm here in the darkness of a prison cell. It's been quite a day, Angus. I'll be glad when this whole thing is over and I can get back to my old routine.

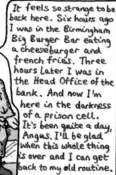

LADY PRESCOTT IN THE MEANTIME HAD CLIMBED THE STEPS TO THE GOVERNOR'S OFFICE. SIR GERALD WAS WAITING NERVOUSLY BY THE DOOR.

HE'D OBVIOUSLY DRESSED UP FOR THE OCCASION, COMBING HIS HAIR, POLISHING HIS SHOES AND PUTTING ON THE SPOTTED PINK TIE THAT LADY PRESCOTT HAD GIVEN HIM ON THEIR SILVER WEDDING ANNIVERSARY.

HISTORY DOES NOT RECORD WHAT ISSUES OF DOMESTIC IMPORTANCE WERE DISCUSSED THAT EVENING IN THE PRESCOTT HOUSEHOLD. BUT THERE IS A RUMOUR THAT THE NEXT MORNING SIR GERALD WENT OUT AND BOUGHT A NEW PAIR OF RUBBER WASHING UP GLOVES AND A BOOK CALLED 'HOW TO FLATTEN YOUR STOMACH AND LOSE YOUR DOUBLE CHIN'.

The story continues...

That weekend, the governor brought the parole forms down to Frederick's cell.

'I owe you a great deal, Mr Carruthers,' he said. 'Your escape was a blessing in disguise. The events of the last twenty-four hours have taught me a lot. I've come to appreciate just how good my life is. Oh, and by the way, my wife has told me all about the kidney machines and the children in the ward. I think you were very brave. I rang up the Home Office last night and we've fixed up your parole. We're going to give you twelve months off for good behaviour! That means we'll be letting you out on Monday.

Now, there's just one more thing that we have to sort out. The other prisoners don't know that you escaped. Angus and I hushed the whole thing up. So, if anyone asks you where you've been for the past twenty-four hours, just say that we thought you'd gone down with German measles. We took you up to the hospital wing and called in a doctor, but it turned out that you had a rash, or an allergy or something, which cleared up overnight. You can make up any story you like. But don't let on that you managed to break out. Otherwise Angus and I will be out of a job.'

Frederick began to laugh. 'Your secret is safe with me, Governor,' he said. 'And anyway, if anyone found out that I ran away, I couldn't get parole. So it's in my interests to hush everything up too!'

◆ ◆ ◆ ◆ ◆ ◆ ◆ ◆

Dawn broke over Newtown Prison. It was Monday, and Frederick Carruthers was going home. Sir Gerald, Lady Prescott and Angus stood by the front gates to see him off. They shook hands and talked for a few minutes. Then the huge iron gates swung open and Frederick walked out onto the street.

It was a strange feeling to be truly free again – like having a canvas and a brush and not knowing what to paint. But Frederick was looking forward to doing the simple things again – walking the dogs after Sunday lunch, browsing in bookshops, fishing in the canal.

The family were there to meet him. They'd stood by him through all the ups and downs of the past two years. And, now, there was so much to say, so much to do. So much lost time to make up for.

◆ ◆ ◆ ◆ ◆ ◆ ◆ ◆

A few days later, a table was reserved at the best Italian restaurant in Newtown. And that night, the Carruthers family, Angus Macpherson and Sir Gerald and Lady Prescott dined out in style.

There was only one topic of conversation – but that's often the way at the best parties. Frederick told the story of the night of his escape – how he had swum across a river, crawled through a field of turnips and jumped on and off trains. Angus described how he'd broken out in a cold sweat when he'd woken up and found out that Frederick had managed to break out and run off. Sir Gerald explained how they'd made up a story that Frederick had gone down with a particularly contagious form of German measles in an attempt to hush up news of the breakout. And Lady Prescott recounted the story of driving into a lay-by and coming across a shabby down-and-out with such a kindly, honest face.

Practice

25

parole	breakout	rash	trains	Frederick
life	coast	river	belt	behaviour

1 The _____ is clear. And Mr Macpherson is waiting for you.

2 Angus took the keys off his _____.

3 I've come to appreciate just how good my _____ is.

4 We're going to give you twelve months off for good _____.

5 But it turned out that you had a _____ or an allergy.

6 If anyone found out that I ran away, I couldn't get _____.

7 Frederick told the story of the night of his escape – how he had swum across a _____

8 ...and jumped on and off _____.

9 Angus had woken up and found out that _____ had managed to break out and run off.

10 Sir Gerald had tried to hush up news of the _____.

26

across	away	off	of	up
out	out	out	on	on

1 Angus took the keys _____ his belt and unlocked cell 269.

2 Don't let _____

3 ...that you managed to break _____.

4 And anyway, if anyone found _____ that

5 ...I ran _____, I couldn't get parole.

6 So it's in my interests to hush everything _____ too!

7 That night, the Carruthers family, Angus Macpherson and Sir Gerald and Lady Prescott dined _____ in style.

8 Frederick told the story _____ the night of his escape –

9 ...how he had swum _____ a river

10 ...and jumped _____ and off trains.

Notes

1 *to dress up* = to make yourself look as smart as possible
You dress up for an interview, meeting, party, etc.

2 Note these three common patterns:
   a *go out and...*
   b *go out to...*
   c *go out for...*

   'Sir Gerald went out and bought a new pair of rubber washing-up gloves...' (Chapter Fourteen)

   ◆ She went out to get some fruit...

   ◆ They went out for a meal...

3 'I owe you a great deal...'
Notice similar collocations such as...

- ◆ I owe you an apology.

- ◆ I owe you £100.

- ◆ I owe you an explanation.

4 *Hush!* = Be quiet!
to hush (something) up   = to keep (something) quiet
= to keep (information) secret

5 In the following sentences, *off* = free.

'Frederick had run across the prison yard, climbed over a wall and run off into the night.' (Chapter Five)

'...the governor would have let you off the last twelve months of your sentence...' (Chapter Thirteen)

'We're going to give you twelve months off for good behaviour!' (Chapter Fourteen)

Note also:

- ◆ We get an hour off for lunch.

- ◆ a day off, a week off, a month off, etc.

6 'We...called in a doctor.' (Chapter Fourteen)
You can also call in a plumber, an engineer or an expert.

7 'We thought you'd gone down with German measles...' (Chapter Fourteen)
You can also go down with flu, mumps, measles and malaria.

8 Note the similarity between *to end up* and *to turn out* – phrasal verbs used when the result is surprising, shocking or unexpected.

'How could a good man end up like this?' (Chapter Twelve)

'But it turned out that you had a rash or something...' (Chapter Fourteen)

CHAPTER FIFTEEN

AT 10.30, JUST AFTER THE FOURTH COURSE, BUT SOME TIME BEFORE THE FIFTH, ANGUS LOOKED AT HIS WATCH AND SIGHED.

I'll have to go now. I'm on duty in half an hour.

HE STOOD UP AND SAID GOODBYE TO MRS CARRUTHERS, THE CHILDREN, SIR GERALD AND LADY PRESCOTT. THEN HE TURNED AND THANKED FREDERICK FOR THE MEAL.

Thank YOU Angus. None of this would have been possible if you hadn't let me escape. You've changed my life. I owe you a lot.

ANGUS BLUSHED A DEEP SHADE OF RED AND LOOKED DOWN AT THE FLOOR. HE DID UP HIS COAT. FREDERICK SMILED AND PATTED HIM ON THE SHOULDER.

All's well that ends well.

ANGUS LEFT THE RESTAURANT AND WALKED BACK ALONG THE PEACEFUL STREETS OF NEWTOWN.

WHEN HE CAME TO THE PRISON GATES HE KNOCKED ON THE FRONT DOOR AND THE NIGHT GUARD LET HIM IN.

ANGUS CLOCKED ON,

PUT ON HIS UNIFORM, AND THEN WENT THROUGH THE CORRIDORS CHECKING THE CELLS AND TURNING OFF THE LIGHTS.

EVERYTHING WAS IN ORDER. THE PRISONERS HAD SETTLED DOWN FOR THE NIGHT AND THE JAIL WAS LOCKED AND STILL.

ANGUS YAWNED AND SAT DOWN ON A SMALL WOODEN BENCH. HE WAS TIRED. AND NOW —AS THE CLOCK STRUCK 11 – THE FRENCH FRIES, THE WELSH RABBIT MADE WITH BLUE CHEESE, THE SCOTCH EGG COVERED WITH FRENCH DRESSING, THE STEAK (WELL DONE) AND THE THREE PLATEFULS OF SPAGHETTI BOLOGNESE HE'D ENJOYED AT DINNER WERE PULLING HIM TOWARDS THE DEEPEST OF DEEP SLEEPS.

I'll just have a little nap. I'm sure nobody will mind if I nod off for a while.

HE STRETCHED OUT, TOOK OFF HIS BELT AND DROPPED IT ONTO THE FLOOR.

A FEW MINUTES LATER THE STONE CORRIDORS ECHOED TO ANGUS MACPHERSON'S UNMISTAKEABLE SNORES.

MEANWHILE, IN THE DARKNESS OF CELL 269, ANGELA RICHARDSON (AN ATHLETE WHO HAD RUN OFF WITH THE MEMBERSHIP FEES OF HER LOCAL SPORTS CLUB) WAS PLANNING HER ESCAPE.

BUT THAT – AS THEY SAY – IS ANOTHER STORY...

Practice

27 Revision Exercise

In Chapters Eleven to Fifteen, who...

	FREDERICK	LADY PRESCOTT	KAREN BLACKSTONE	ANGUS	SIR GERALD
1 ...was falling apart?					
2 ...looked up a number?					
3 ...looked out at Crawford Street?					
4 ...nodded off in the blue Rolls Royce?					
5 ...looked like a scarecrow in a thunderstorm?					
6 ...went through Frederick's file?					
7 ...threw away thirty years of hard work?					
8 ...showed up the flaws in the bank's security system?					
9 ...butted in?					
10 ...was due for parole?					
11 ...was waiting for Frederick?					
12 ...took the keys off his belt?					
13 ...sat down?					
14 ...put on a spotted pink tie?					
15 ...stood up?					
16 ...clocked on?					
17 ...put on his uniform?					
18 ...went through the corridors?					
19 ...turned off the lights?					
20 ...nodded off in Newtown Prison?					

Notes

1 *to do up* (your coat, shirt, jacket, top button, etc.) is the opposite of *to undo* (your coat, shirt, jacket, top button, etc.)

2 *to go through* = to check

Compare...

'Angus went through the corridors checking the cells...' (Chapter Fifteen)

and

'The Head of Finance went to the central computer and started going through my account.' (Chapter Eleven)

3 *Welsh rabbit* = cheese on toast

4 *to run off with (something)* = to steal (something) and then run away

CHAPTER ONE

Practice

On a cold November evening many years ago, Angus Macpherson (chief guard at the Newtown Prison) yawned and closed his eyes.

Angus had had a long and tiring day and now, as the clock struck eleven, the three platefuls of spaghetti bolognese he'd enjoyed at dinner were pulling him towards the deepest of deep sleeps.

'I'll just have a little nap,' he thought to himself. 'All the cells are locked and everything's quiet. I'm sure nobody will mind if I nod __1__ for a while.'

Angus stretched __2__ on a wooden bench and tried to relax. But, for some reason, he couldn't get off to sleep. Then he had an idea. 'I know what the trouble is,' he said to himself. 'It's this belt of mine. It's much too tight.'

He rolled __3__ , took __4__ the belt and dropped it __5__ the floor.

A few minutes later, the stone corridors echoed to Angus Macpherson's unmistakable snore.

In the darkness of cell 269, Frederick Carruthers (a bank manager who had lent himself £250,000) was planning his escape.

'If I could get the keys __6__ Macpherson's belt,' he said to himself, 'I could slip __7__ through the side door, run __8__ the yard, jump __9__ the prison wall and be back home for breakfast. But how do I do it?'

Just then, he caught sight of Angus's belt lying __10__ the floor. 'The keys!' Carruthers whispered. 'He's just dropped the belt with the keys. This is too good to be true.'

He tiptoed to the front of his cell and looked __11__ . There was no one __12__ . He took a deep breath. And then, softly and slowly, he stretched __13__ his hand, picked __14__ the belt and lifted it back through the bars...

♦ ♦ ♦ ♦ ♦ ♦ ♦ ♦ ♦ ♦ ♦ ♦ ♦

CHAPTER TWO

Practice

Dawn broke over Newtown Prison. Angus stretched, yawned and half opened his eyes. 'I feel much better now,' he said to himself. 'I think that little nap did me good.'

He stood __15__ and looked __16__ his belt. But, for some reason, it wasn't on the floor where he'd dropped it. He yawned again and thought about going back to sleep. But then, to his surprise, he suddenly saw his belt hanging on a key which was in the lock of the open door of cell 269.

Angus blinked twice. 'Something's wrong here!' he said to himself. 'But what is it?'

Gradually, shockingly, horrifyingly, the awful truth dawned on him.

When Angus had at last worked __17__ what had happened, he rushed down the corridor and ran __18__ the steps to the prison governor's office. With his heart pounding, he banged on the door. 'Governor, Governor!' he shouted. 'Let me in! Let me in!'

Sir Gerald Prescott was sitting __19__ his desk, reading *The Times*.

'Come __20__ ,' he said. 'The door's open.'

Angus rushed __21__ , his red face covered with sweat.

'What's the matter, Macpherson?' the prison governor asked. 'You look a bit upset.'

'It's Frederick Carruthers,' Angus shouted. 'He's broken out of his cell and run away, and it was all my fault!'

'Now calm __22__ ,' Sir Gerald said. 'And go __23__ the whole story very slowly right from the start.'

Angus sat down and took a deep breath. 'Well, Sir,' he began. 'Last night I stretched __24__ on a wooden bench near cell 269. I took __25__ my belt and dropped it onto the floor. Then I nodded __26__ for a few minutes.

While I was asleep, Carruthers stretched out his hand, picked __27__ the belt and took off one of the keys. He opened his cell and slipped out through the side door.'

'But that's terrible!' the prison governor screamed, tearing __28__ his *Times* and bursting __29__ tears.

Angus took a handkerchief out of his pocket and handed it to Sir Gerald. 'Now, now, Sir,' he said. 'There's no need to cry. It wasn't your fault that Carruthers escaped. I shouldn't have taken __30__ my belt and nodded __31__ like that. But don't worry, Governor! I'll make up __32__ it. I'll give __33__ my lunchbreak and go out and look __34__ him and find __35__ where he is.'

◆ ◆ ◆ ◆ ◆ ◆ ◆ ◆ ◆ ◆ ◆ ◆ ◆ ◆

CHAPTER THREE

Practice

At that moment, Lady Prescott, the wife of the prison governor, arrived.

'For goodness sake stop crying, Gerald,' she said, taking __36__ her coat. 'Pull yourself together man! What's wrong with you? Why don't you grow __37__ ?'

'I can't help it,' the governor replied. 'Yet another of my prisoners has run away. That's the fifth one this week. Why don't they like it here? Is it the prison food? Or the colour of the walls? Or my after-shave? I wish I knew.' And with that he burst __38__ tears again.

'That's it,' Lady Prescott said, putting __39__ her coat. 'I've had enough of all this nonsense. I hate to see a grown man cry and I'm not going to put up __40__ it any longer. I'm leaving you, Gerald! I'm going to break up our marriage and run __41__ to a run-down area of Birmingham.'

'But you can't do that!' the prison governor cried. 'If you run away to a run-__42__ area of Birmingham, I'll have a nervous breakdown.'

'That's your problem, not mine,' Lady Prescott replied. 'I'm going to walk out of that door and you'll never see me again!'

'But I won't let you go!' Sir Gerald shouted. 'If you run away, I'll run __43__ you.'

'If I run away to a run- __44__ area and you run __45__ me,' Lady Prescott replied, 'I'll run over you in my car.'

'OUR car,' the governor corrected her. 'You should remember that we bought it together. But you must be careful, my dear. If you run away to a run- __46__ area of Birmingham and I run __47__ you and you run __48__ me in the car, you might then run into a tree, and the cost of repairing the damage could run __49__ hundreds of pounds.'

'Money! Money! Money! That's all you care about!' Lady Prescott screamed. 'Here am I threatening to break __50__ our marriage and run __51__ to a run-__52__ area of Birmingham, and all you can think __53__ is the cost of repairing the car – OUR car – if you run __54__ me and I run __55__ you and then run __56__ a tree! That's so typical of you! Self! Self! Self! Me! Me! Me! I've had enough. I've run __57__ of patience, Gerald. I'm off.'

◆ ◆ ◆ ◆ ◆ ◆ ◆ ◆ ◆ ◆ ◆ ◆ ◆

CHAPTER FOUR

Practice

'No, No, No. You can't do this to me,' the prison governor shouted, kneeling down and bursting __58__ tears. 'Look, I know I've not been a very good husband lately. I've been working too hard and putting __59__ weight. But you can't walk out on me like this. If you went away, I'd go to pieces. I know what the problem is! I've been so wrapped up in my work that I've started to take you for granted. But don't leave me. Give me one last chance. I'll make __60__ for it! I'll be putty in your hands. You name it and I'll do it. I'll take up jogging and take __61__ weight! I'll give __62__ smoking and wash __63__ after dinner! I'll clear out the cupboards and take you out at weekends. Now what could be fairer than that?'

Lady Prescott turned __64__, threw an ashtray __65__ Sir Gerald, knocked __66__ a chair and stormed __67__ of the room.

'Shall I go after her?' Angus asked from somewhere behind the armchair.

'No,' Sir Gerald replied softly, picking __68__ the ashtray and putting it back on the table. 'Let her go. She's made __69__ her mind to run __70__ to a run-__71__ area of Birmingham, and there's nothing we can do.'

The prison governor sat __72__ and straightened his tie.

'I don't know what's got __73__ her lately,' he said, shaking his head. 'She used to be so calm and quiet. But now she blows __74__ all the time. I can't understand women, Angus. I just can't make them __75__. Why can't they be strong and logical like us men?'

And, with that, Sir Gerald took a handkerchief out of his pocket, blew his nose and, not for the first time, burst __76__ tears.

◆ ◆ ◆ ◆ ◆ ◆ ◆ ◆ ◆ ◆ ◆ ◆ ◆ ◆

CHAPTER FIVE

Practice

By the time that Lady Prescott had stormed __77__ of the office, and Sir Gerald had straightened his tie, and Angus had come out from behind the armchair, Frederick Carruthers was well on his way home.

After he had slipped __78__ through the side door, Frederick had run __79__ the prison yard, climbed over a wall and run off into the night.

Having crossed the main road that links Newtown to Oldtown, he had rolled down a hill, climbed over a couple of gates, crawled __80__ a field full of turnips, waded __81__ a swamp, dived into a stream and swum __82__ to the opposite bank, climbed up a hill, run across six kilometres of open countryside, jumped onto a train that was slowing down in front of a set of signals, run down the corridor to avoid the ticket collector and then jumped __83__ again as the train pulled into a station.

While the other passengers were getting __84__ the train, Frederick had slipped __85__ the ticket barrier by showing his prison identification badge and shouting, 'I'm a train engineer. I'm a train engineer. Let me through. Let me through!'

Then he'd elbowed his way __86__ a group of tourists, rushed down a flight of steps, run __87__ a subway tunnel and, finally, ended up standing outside a cafe at a lay-by near Junction 34 of the M1 motorway.

It was at this moment that his problems really began. Frederick had been rushing, rolling, running, jumping, climbing, crawling, wading and swimming for several hours now and the last meal he'd had was three biscuits and a glass of water before Angus had turned __88__ the light in his cell. His exhausted body was beginning to complain. His stomach was crying out for food and his throat felt like sandpaper. But what could he do? Prisoners don't carry money and he didn't have a penny __89__ him.

Frederick looked through the windows of the cafe and for the next few moments he went through a dreadful torture. 'What have I done to deserve this?' he thought. 'Here am I – with my stomach rumbling and my throat parched, and I can't even afford a cup of tea! How did I get into this mess? And, more to the point, how do I get out of it?'

These were the thoughts running __90__ Frederick Carruthers' troubled mind as a blue Rolls Royce pulled into the lay-by and glided to a halt.

♦ ♦ ♦ ♦ ♦ ♦ ♦ ♦ ♦ ♦ ♦ ♦ ♦

CHAPTER SIX

Practice

The blue Rolls Royce glided to a halt a few metres from where Frederick was standing. The driver wound down her window and leaned __91__.

'Excuse me,' she said. 'Do you know anything about cars? I'm having a few problems with the steering and I think I may have a puncture. Could you take a look for me?'

'Yes, of course,' Frederick said, and through his mind went the simple formula: 'Changing a wheel is work. Work brings money. Money brings food.'

The front left-hand wheel was hissing like a snake. Frederick bent down and ran his hand over the tyre. 'You were lucky,' he said. 'This is a slow puncture. It could have been a lot worse.'

Then he pulled a large piece of glass __92__ of the wheel and held it up. 'That's what caused the problem,' he said. 'You must have picked it up along the way.'

Frederick walked to the back of the car and opened up the boot. Then he took __93__ the spare wheel, a tool kit, a jack and a pump. He took __94__ his jacket, hung it up on one of the wing mirrors, jacked up the car, took __95__ the flat tyre, put __96__ the spare wheel which he then pumped up a little, and finally, having done all that, he put the old wheel, the tool kit, the jack and the pump back in the boot.

'You've been so kind,' the lady said.

Frederick nodded, smiled and held __97__ his hand.

'Now, can I give you a lift anywhere? I'm on my way to Birmingham. Would that be any good for you? Perhaps I can drop you off somewhere along the way.'

Frederick's face dropped. He'd been expecting money or food and he felt a bit let down. But then it suddenly dawned __98__ him that the offer of a free ride in a Rolls Royce far away from Newtown might be quite a good idea.

'That's very kind of you,' he said, wiping his hands on a cloth and getting into the car. 'Birmingham would be just fine.'

The woman got in, put __99__ her seat belt, took off the handbrake, put the car into first gear, looked in the rear-view mirror, and pulled gently __100__ of the lay-by. And then – with a sudden burst of speed – they roared __101__ the M1 motorway like a bullet from a gun.

◆ ◆ ◆ ◆ ◆ ◆ ◆ ◆ ◆ ◆ ◆ ◆ ◆

CHAPTER SEVEN

Practice

'The steering's fine now,' the lady said, as the blue Rolls Royce sped __102__ down the M1. 'I'm very grateful to you, Mr...er...'

'Carruthers, Frederick Carruthers.'

'Now that name rings a bell,' the woman said. 'I'm sure I've come __103__ it somewhere before. But I can't quite place it. And so, tell me, Mr Carruthers, what do you do?'

Frederick paused. He looked __104__ of the window and waved his hand in a rather vague way. 'I... er... I'm in prisons,' he said.

'Well I never! Isn't that a coincidence!' the woman replied. 'So is my husband. Perhaps you've heard __105__ him. His name is Sir Gerald Prescott.'

Frederick sank lower in his seat. 'Your husband?' he said, as a cold shiver ran __106__ his spine. 'Your husband is Sir Gerald Prescott? The governor of Newtown Jail?'

'That's right!' the woman replied. 'Do you know him?'

'Er... not personally,' Frederick said. 'But I... em... know __107__ him... He has quite a reputation in my field.'

'Does he? Does he indeed?' the driver said, with a soft and bitter laugh. 'Well, I'm sure it's a reputation for childish, incompetent stupidity! My husband has the intelligence of a pineapple and the imagination of a do-nut.'

Lady Prescott's voice grew louder as she warmed to her subject. 'Sir Gerald is the weakest, the stupidest, the meanest and the most selfish man to walk this earth.'

Frederick wanted to move on to another topic like the weather or the price of cauliflowers, but it was no good. Lady Prescott was getting carried away and there was just no stopping her now.

'Sir Gerald's nickname is Niagara because he keeps bursting __108__ tears,' she screamed, like a dragon breathing fire. 'When I first met him he was a tiger, but he's turned __109__ a kitten. He's a stubborn, ignorant jelly and he drives me __110__ the wall.'

Frederick sat in a state of shock, trying to squeeze words through his frozen lips. But it was just no good. His mouth opened and closed like a demented goldfish. And although he did manage a few incoherent grunts, none of the sounds came out right. So – recognising defeat – he gave up trying to change the subject, sat __111__ and just watched the volcano erupt.

Frederick's mind was not at peace. Here he was sitting __112__ a Rolls Royce driven by the wife of the governor of the prison he'd just escaped __113__. He was mumbling, his stomach was rumbling, his confidence was crumbling, and Lady Prescott was grumbling.

'Perhaps I should have stayed in my cell,' he thought, as the driver put her foot down and the blue Rolls Royce roared __114__ .

◆ ◆ ◆ ◆ ◆ ◆ ◆ ◆ ◆ ◆ ◆ ◆

CHAPTER EIGHT

Practice

By the time they arrived at the outskirts of Birmingham, Lady Prescott had calmed __115__ a little and Frederick was feeling a bit more relaxed.

And, as we pick __116__ the story again (at 1.23 p.m.), our two characters have started to get __117__ surprisingly well...

◆ ◆ ◆ ◆ ◆ ◆ ◆ ◆ ◆

The blue Rolls Royce slowed __118__ and they drew __119__ in front of a row of shabby terraced houses.

'Do you see number 42, the one with the pale green door?' Lady Prescott said. 'I was born there. And this little run-__120__ street on the edge of the city is where I grew __121__. Whenever I feel __122__, I come __123__ here. This will always be my home. It's dirty and messy and some of the shops are boarded __124__. But as far as I'm concerned, this is the best place in the world.'

Lady Prescott put __125__ the handbrake, took __126__ her seat belt and stepped __127__ of the car. 'And now, Mr Carruthers, I'm going for a walk,' she said. 'Would you like me to show __128__?'

'That would be very kind of you,' Frederick replied. 'But I don't want to put you to any trouble.'

'It would be no trouble at all,' Lady Prescott said. 'In fact, you'd be doing me a favour. I've got a lot of things on my mind at the moment and I need someone to talk to. So I'd be very grateful if you came and walked with me.'

Lady Prescott locked the car and they set __129__ across the market square on a tour of the town.

'Has it changed much over the years?' Frederick asked, as they came __130__ the narrow stone bridge that crossed the canal.

'No, not really,' Lady Prescott replied. 'They've done __131__ some of the houses...like these ones here... but most of the properties are falling __132__ or falling __133__. Whenever there's an election, the politicians come __134__ and knock __135__ the door. They promise to pull __136__ the terraced housing and build some new flats. But after the votes are counted, they never seem to get __137__ to it. It's strange that, isn't it?

And – anyway – I'd be a bit sad if they knocked everything __138__ and put __139__ one of those ugly tower blocks. Perhaps it's better to keep it the way it is. I don't want them tearing __140__ my childhood. They should leave my home alone.'

'You say this is your home,' Frederick said. 'But then why did you go __141__?'

'Oh, that's simple,' Lady Prescott replied. 'I fell in love. Strange though it may seem, I left Birmingham to be with Gerald Prescott – the gutless, brainless, spineless fool who is now governor of Newtown Prison. You look a bit surprised, Mr Carruthers. Then perhaps I should explain.

There was a time when my husband was a bright, tender young man. It's only recently that he's turned __142__ a workaholic who eats, drinks and sleeps prison life.

I met him when I was just eighteen. I was in my last term at school and Gerald was studying at the local technical college. He was absolutely broke and so he'd taken a part-time job at a take-away restaurant called The Birmingham Big Burger Bar. The take-away was in Crawford Street. It was on my way home from school. One day, I went __143__ to get some chips. Gerald was serving behind the counter. He smiled __144__ me and I felt a cold shiver run __145__ my spine.

After that, I went to the take-away every day. I wasn't hungry. I just wanted to see Gerald. Anyway, one afternoon he asked me __146__ and we went for a walk in the park. We got __147__ really well and I started seeing him all the time. He used to walk me __148__ school in the morning and he'd come and pick me __149__ when the classes were over. And then – all of a sudden – I fell __150__ love with him. I don't know why. It just happened that way.

When my father found __151__ what was going __152__, he went crazy. He didn't want his only daughter going __153__ with someone who cooked hamburgers in a take-away. He told me that I had to stop seeing Gerald straightaway.

I had to make a choice. Should I obey my father and split __154__ with the person I loved? Or should I defy my parents and go __155__ seeing him? It didn't take me long to make __156__ my mind! I knew that I couldn't give Gerald __157__. And so I had to work __158__ some way of deceiving my parents.

The plan was simple. I pretended that I'd obeyed my father. I said that I'd broken __159__ with Gerald. I cried for two or three days and went __160__ ten packets of tissues. I stopped eating and slammed lots of doors. I put __161__ a really good show. My parents were completely taken __162__.

But whenever my father's back was turned, I would slip __163__ of the house and go and meet Gerald secretly, in the park or at the take-away. When I came home, I made __164__ some story or other to explain where I'd been. "I was at a friend's house playing records" or "I was visiting a museum in the centre of the town".

My father seemed happy that I'd suddenly made lots of new friends who had money in their pockets and didn't cook burgers. But he didn't know what I was really __165__ to...'

Lady Prescott suddenly broke __166__ and – for the next minute or so – they walked __167__ in silence. Frederick looked straight ahead. He said nothing. There was no need to talk. They crossed a main road and walked past a school. And then, as they turned __168__ a narrow side street, Lady Prescott picked __169__ the story again...

◆ ◆ ◆ ◆ ◆ ◆ ◆ ◆ ◆ ◆ ◆ ◆ ◆ ◆

CHAPTER NINE

Practice

On my last day at school, Gerald asked me to marry him. As you can imagine, I felt tremendously flattered. But I turned him __170__. I told him I was just too young to settle __171__. I needed more time to think things __172__. For the next few months we played a sort of game. He kept __173__ proposing and I kept __174__ saying "no".

But then one night – it was May 10th – everything changed. I told my father I was going to a poetry reading in the local Town Hall. In fact, I slipped __175__ of the side door and went to the cinema with Gerald. When the film was over, we caught the last bus home but – along the way – the bus broke __176__ and all the passengers had to get __177__ and walk.

It was four miles from the city centre __178__ my house and by the time we got home, it was very late. Gerald saw me to the door, kissed me on the cheek and then said goodnight.

It was now two o'clock in the morning. I took __179__ my key and let myself __180__ as quietly as I could. My father was waiting for me in the hall. He normally went to bed at about eleven but – that night – he'd decided to stay __181__ until I got __182__.

He was furious. He'd seen Gerald bringing me to the door and – at that moment – he'd realised what had been going __183__ behind his back. I'd never seen my father so angry. I thought he was going to hit me! So, I ran past him and went straight up to bed.

The next morning at breakfast, we had a huge row. He shouted at me. I shouted at him. And it ended up with me packing a suitcase and storming __184__ of the house. I went straight round to Gerald's flat and we decided to run __185__. Can you imagine it? Me and Gerald running __186__!

Anyway, to cut a long story short, we eloped to Newtown and got married in the local church. It was a very quiet wedding. Just me, Gerald, the vicar and a couple of witnesses. All very romantic!

As soon as the service was over, I rang up my parents to tell them what we'd done. My father was stunned and hurt. He lost his temper and slammed down the phone. For the next few months, we went __187__ a really bad patch. I didn't go back to the house and whenever I rang home there were long pregnant pauses. It was all very awkward.

But then one day, Gerald went __188__ to see my father. They had a long talk and – somehow – they sorted the whole thing __189__. I made it __190__ with my parents, and since then, we've been very close.

And I suppose that now – looking back – I can appreciate what my mother and father were going __191__. I was their only daughter and they didn't think my husband was good enough for me. After all, when Gerald was younger, he wasn't exactly rolling in money. He was so hard __192__ that he'd use the same tea bag for a week. He owned three socks and they all had holes in them. His shirt sleeves were frayed and his trousers were held __193__ with string.'

Lady Prescott sighed and smiled. A single tear ran down her cheek. 'Ah, those were happy days,' she said.

Lady Prescott broke off and – once again – they walked on in silence.

It was now mid-afternoon and the streets were empty. There was a stillness in the cool summer air, as if the world had paused for thought. No birds sang. No cows mooed. No ducks quacked. No sheep baaed. No dogs woofed. No cats miaowed. In fact, on that bright, soft, tranquil day there was only one sound to be heard – the low, continuous rumbling of Frederick's empty stomach, for twenty-four hours starved of food.

They walked down a couple of alleyways and then, as they turned __194__ the main road, they came upon a postman riding a bicycle. The bicycle was very old and it had no springs. And so as he rode across the cobblestones, he seemed to be nodding his head and shaking his head all at the same time.

Lady Prescott was talking again: 'Do you know where we are, Mr Carruthers? This is Crawford Street. And at the end of this row of shops, there's The Birmingham Big Burger Bar – where I met Gerald all those years ago. Look, I don't know about you, but I'm starving. Why don't we pop in there and have a late lunch? They serve the best beefburgers in town!'

Frederick seemed a little agitated. 'I could do with a meal too,' he said. 'But I'm afraid I don't have a penny __195__ me. You see, I went out in rather a hurry last night.'

Lady Prescott smiled. 'But you must be my guest, Mr Carruthers. You've gone out of your way to help me and you've put __196__ with all my complaints about Sir Gerald. Paying __197__ lunch will be my way of paying you back for all your kindness. Come __198__, I insist. I've had a long and difficult day. I'm tired __199__ and very worked __200__ about my husband. I need a good meal to calm me down and I don't want to eat alone.'

◆ ◆ ◆ ◆ ◆ ◆ ◆ ◆ ◆ ◆ ◆ ◆ ◆ ◆ ◆

Chapter ten

Practice

Lady Prescott was right about the food. It was definitely the best burger that Frederick had ever tasted. But that was hardly surprising. He was so hungry that he could have eaten the serviettes and the cheap blue plastic tray.

Lady Prescott looked **201** her watch. 'It's three o'clock,' she said. 'I've been rabbiting **202** about my problems for over an hour now. Look, I'm sorry. I didn't mean to burden you. It's just that after my bust-up with Sir Gerald, I suppose I needed someone to talk to.'

She paused. There was something on her mind.

'Mr Carruthers, I want to ask you a question,' she began, her voice now somewhat colder than before. 'When I drove into that lay-by, you were standing **203** with your hands in your pockets looking like a down-and-out. But you have an honest, kindly face and you're obviously an intelligent man. So how did you end **204** like that? There must be something wrong. And I think it's time for you to tell me the truth. Why were you wandering **205** near the motorway with no money in your pocket and those very strange clothes?'

Frederick said nothing. He looked down at the table and stirred his coffee with a spoon. He didn't know what to do. He wanted to explain things, but he wasn't sure whether he could trust Lady Prescott. After all, she was the wife of the governor of the prison he'd just escaped from. If she found **206** that he was a convict on the run, perhaps she'd turn him **207** . And then he might end up in cell 269 again.

Frederick looked up. 'You're right of course,' he said, breaking the silence. 'It *is* strange that I should be drifting **208** with nowhere to go. And yes, I am in trouble. But if I told you what I've gone through in the past few months, you might get angry. And that would make things worse.'

Lady Prescott finished **209** her French fries and smiled.

'You've no reason to be afraid,' she said. 'If you're in trouble, then you need help. And if there's something on your mind, you shouldn't just bottle it **210** inside you. You should tell me about it and get it **211** your chest. Then you'd feel a lot better. And I give you my word that I won't get angry, whatever you say.'

Frederick sighed. 'Perhaps you're right,' he said. 'And, after all, what have I got to lose? Well, the truth is that up until two years ago, I was leading a very simple and predictable life. I had a steady job, a beautiful home and a loving family. Then, all of a sudden, something happened that changed everything. My whole world just fell apart.'

Frederick broke off. He seemed a little uneasy.

'Go on,' Lady Prescott said gently.

'Well, it's a very long story,' Frederick replied. 'And I don't really know where to begin.'

'Try the beginning,' said Lady Prescott, putting a straw into her milkshake. 'I'm in no hurry. I'm going to drink this very, very slowly.'

Frederick took a deep breath and picked up the story again. 'My mother is a nurse in a small hospital,' he said. 'She looks **212** sick children. She's a wonderful, extraordinary woman and she works incredibly hard.

One day, I drove down to the hospital to pick my mother up after work. We were going out to dinner. I parked the car and, as I was walking __213__ one of the wards, I could hear a child crying very softly. I looked __214__ and saw a little boy. He must have been about eight or nine. He was so ill that he couldn't sit __215__ in bed properly. He had to lie against pillows all day long. It was terrible. He was pale, lifeless, too weak to move.

The next day, I rang up the manager of the hospital and asked about the little boy. She told me that all the children in that ward had problems with their kidneys.

"And is there nothing you can do?" I asked.

"I'm afraid not," she said. "What we really need is half a dozen kidney machines. Then the children would be able to get __216__ of bed and walk __217__ the ward. But, unfortunately, the hospital is very short of money. We're so hard __218__ that we can't afford to buy one machine, let alone six. So, I'm afraid the children will just have to suffer."

When I put down the phone, I felt terribly disturbed. It was so sad, so shocking, so unfair. I decided that I had to find a way to help the children. I couldn't stand by and do nothing.

At first, I couldn't think what to do. But then – all of a sudden – I came __219__ with an idea. I was a bank manager and a lot of money passed __220__ my hands. During a normal working day, I would write out ten, maybe twelve, official cheques for different things – stationery, coffee, furniture, stamps, and so on. I'd worked at the bank for thirty years, so everybody knew me. And nobody ever checked __221__ on what I was doing. I suppose I had an honest face and they just trusted me!

One afternoon – it was a Wednesday – I called my secretary into the office and told her to cancel my appointments. When she'd left the room, I took the phone off the hook and drew the curtains. Then I took the official cheque book out of the safe and wrote a cheque to myself!

```
Pay Mr F. Carruthers,
£100.00 only
Signed Frederick Carruthers.
```

It was breathtakingly, outrageously simple. A bank manager stealing money from his own bank!

◆ ◆ ◆ ◆ ◆ ◆ ◆ ◆ ◆ ◆ ◆ ◆ ◆ ◆

CHAPTER ELEVEN

Practice

At the age of forty-five, I was about to commit my first crime. I looked __222__ the cheque. My head was spinning. This was robbery. Was I doing the right thing? Could I get away with it? Should I just tear __223__ the cheque and throw it away? Perhaps I should forget about the whole thing.

But then I thought __224__ the children in the hospital. They needed the money more than the bank. I was stealing it for them.

So, I took a deep breath, folded the cheque __225__ and put it into my pocket.

I left the office and took a taxi to another branch of the bank. I knew one of the cashiers there. We chatted for a while. And then, with my heart pounding, I paid the cheque into my current account. Three days later, the payment cleared. I had stolen my first £100.

The following week, I did the whole thing again. Another cheque. The same branch. The same cashier. The same fear. The same excitement when the money was cleared into my account.

And so it went __226__. Week after week, I stole money from the bank and each cheque was a little bigger than the last.

You've no idea how I felt. I was risking everything I had – my career, my family life, my reputation. But nothing was going to stop me now. The image of the little boy crying on his pillow haunted me. I couldn't get it out of my mind. And I had to do something to help.

I think the next few weeks were the most exciting of my life. In some strange way, I'd suddenly come alive. I was sharp, human, burning with anger. And I suppose I got a bit carried away.

I was soon writing cheques for five and ten thousand pounds. It was crazy. Sometimes, the cashier seemed a bit suspicious. She couldn't work __227__ what the payments were for. But – each week – I made __228__ some new story to explain the cheques away. And she fell for it every time. I suppose it never occurred to her that Frederick Carruthers – her punctual, conscientious friend – could have turned into a common thief, an embezzler, a liar, a man obsessed. By that summer, I'd managed to save __229__ a quarter of a million pounds.

One morning, I didn't go into work. I walked into the hospital and wrote out a cheque for every penny I had. The manager went straight out and bought six new kidney machines.

A few days later, we had a small ceremony in the ward. It was a bit like launching a ship, or opening a bridge! I unwrapped the machines, plugged them in and switched them __230__. And then, as the lights flashed, the children gave me a round of applause that seemed to go on forever. I felt very proud. It was the best moment of my life.

But then – inevitably, I suppose – my luck failed.

Someone at Head Office became suspicious. How could a branch manager afford to donate £250,000 to a hospital?

The Head of Finance went to the central computer and started going __231__ my account. She noticed that I'd been building up large amounts of cash. But how could I save __232__ so much money on the salary I earned? She smelt a rat and, when she looked into the strange dealings on the branch account, she knew that something was wrong.

Anyway, it wasn't long before she'd put two and two together and worked __233__ what I'd been __234__ to. She tipped __235__ the police and, when I turned up for work the next morning, there were three detectives waiting in my office. They took me down to the police station and that was it. I was charged with theft and my world just fell __236__. The trial was fixed for December 18th – just one week before Christmas!

Two days before I was due in court, a director of the bank came to see me. He came straight to the point. He offered me a deal. He said they would drop all the charges if I paid the money back.

"But how can I do that?" I asked. "The hospital have spent it all."

"That's simple," the man said. "Tell the hospital that you've changed your mind. Tell them it was a mistake. Just tell them to send the machines back."

"But what about the children?" I said.

The man shrugged his shoulders. "Our bank is a business, Mr Carruthers. It's not a charity. And if you don't get our money back, you'll end up in jail. It's as simple as that. It's up to you. But you can't have it both ways."

He stood up. "We're going to give you twenty-four hours to think it __237__," he said. "You don't have to decide right away. You can sleep on it. I'll come back tomorrow and you can tell me what you've decided. But just remember one thing, Mr Carruthers. You can't rip the bank __238__ and expect to get away with it. Life's not like that. And we will hunt you down until we get every penny of our money back. I trust I've made myself clear. Good afternoon."

That night, I lay awake in my cell and thought the whole thing __239__. Was I being stupid? Should I save my own skin? Was it all worth fighting for? I went over it again and again.

The man from the bank came back the next day. He walked into my cell with a stupid smirk on his face. He was so sure of himself. So confident. He thought I was going to give in without a fight. He sat down and grinned __240__ me. And at that moment, I noticed he had false teeth.

"So, Mr Carruthers," he began. "I trust that you've come to your senses. I've prepared this letter for you to sign. It instructs the hospital to send the items in question back to the factory and..."

I held __241__ my hand and the man from the bank stopped talking.

"You can save your breath," I said. "Put the letter away. I've got no intention of signing it. I've decided to go __242__ with the trial. I can't let the children down. I promised them six kidney machines and I'm not going back on my word."

The man from the bank gaped at me and his false teeth fell out. They crashed noisily onto the floor and rolled under my bed. I bent down, picked them __243__ and handed them back to him.

"I believe these are yours," I said. You should have seen his face!

And so the trial went ahead. I pleaded guilty, the judge sentenced me to three years in jail and that's how I ended __244__ in...' Frederick paused and took a deep breath, '...in Newtown Prison... from where I escaped at eleven o'clock last night.'

Lady Prescott blinked twice. She didn't seem at all shocked or upset by the fact that Frederick was a convict on the run from her husband's jail. In fact, her one and only concern was for the children in the ward.

◆ ◆ ◆ ◆ ◆ ◆ ◆ ◆ ◆ ◆ ◆ ◆ ◆

CHAPTER TWELVE

Practice

'There's one thing I don't understand,' Lady Prescott said. 'Why didn't you tell the court what you did with the money? Then they would have seen things in a different light. They would have reduced your sentence. They might even have let you off.'

'I thought of that,' Frederick replied. 'But then the judge would have ordered the hospital to sell the machines and pay the money back. And that was the last thing I wanted. I may have got __245__ of going to prison, but what would have happened to the children? I couldn't take that risk.'

Lady Prescott shook her head. 'I can't decide if you were very brave or very stupid,' she said. 'But I have to admire what you did. And you nearly got away with it. You were really quite unlucky. Now I don't condone stealing. Theft is theft and you deserve to be punished. But after two years in jail, you've paid __246__ your debt.'

A silence fell between them. Frederick was staring deep into his coffee. Telling the story of the kidney machines had brought back some painful memories. And he suddenly felt very down.

'How could a good man end up like this?' Lady Prescott thought. 'He's falling __247__. I must help him. I can't just stand by and do nothing.'

And with that, she suddenly stood __248__ and picked __249__ her bag. 'Would you excuse me, Mr Carruthers?' she said. 'I have a couple of calls to make.'

Lady Prescott walked over to the pay-phone in the corner of the room. She took a yellow diary out of the bag and looked up a number. Then she picked __250__ the receiver, put some coins into the slot and started dialling.

Frederick turned his face and looked __251__ at Crawford Street. There were now lots of people about. It was half past three and the local school had just broken __252__ for the day. A young girl came in and ordered some chips.

Lady Prescott finished her first call and put down the phone. Then she turned __253__ and looked across at Frederick. He was miles away, staring out of the window. She picked __254__ the phone again and dialled a second number.

A few minutes later, she was __255__. 'Is that Newtown Prison?' she whispered. 'This is Lady Prescott. I want to speak to my husband.'

◆ ◆ ◆ ◆ ◆ ◆ ◆ ◆ ◆

Lady Prescott came __256__ to the table and sat down. 'I made a call to a friend of mine, Mr Carruthers. She'd like to meet you. I said we'd be in her office just after five. So why don't you drink __257__ your coffee and eat __258__ your cheeseburger and finish __259__ the French fries and then we can set off.'

'But where are we going?' Frederick said. 'And who is your friend?'

'For the moment, that must remain a secret,' Lady Prescott replied. 'But she's an important woman and I think she can help you. Oh, and do cheer __260__, Mr Carruthers. You mustn't worry so much. It'll all work __261__ in the end.'

Frederick drank __262__ his coffee, ate __263__ his cheeseburger, finished __264__ his French fries and then stood up.

They walked back to the car – along Crawford Street, down a couple of side alleys, over the stone bridge that crossed the canal. And a few minutes later, blue Rolls Royce was on the road again.

Frederick was exhausted. The last twenty-four hours were beginning to catch up with him. And as the car sped __265__ down the motorway, he closed his eyes and gently nodded __266__ , falling ever deeper into sleep.

◆ ◆ ◆ ◆ ◆ ◆ ◆ ◆

A couple of hours later, Frederick felt someone tapping on his shoulder. 'Come along, Mr Carruthers,' Lady Prescott said. 'Wake up. We're nearly there.'

Frederick woke __267__ with a start. And at first he thought he was still dreaming. Because there – right ahead of them – was a vast glass and metal building that he knew all too well. But this was no dream. And their car was heading straight for the main entrance.

'Where are you taking me?' Frederick shouted. 'This is the Head Office of my old bank. You've set me __268__ , haven't you? You're going to turn me in! I should never have trusted you. Stop the car right now! Let me __269__ !'

Frederick took __270__ his seat belt and tried to get out of the car. But Lady Prescott turned round and dragged him back inside.

'For goodness sake, calm down, Mr Carruthers,' she said. 'I haven't set you __271__ and I'm not going to turn you in. And don't get so worked __272__ . You're as bad as my husband. Now, just listen to me. When we were in the take-away, I rang up your Head Office and fixed up an appointment with Karen Blackstone. She's a good friend of mine. We went to school together.'

'Karen Blackstone?' Frederick said. 'But she's the Managing Director of the bank.'

'Exactly, Mr Carruthers. And we're on our way to her office. She's going to give you a new job.'

'You must be joking,' said Frederick. 'The bank would never dream of taking me on again. I've got a criminal record for stealing their money.'

'Well, just you wait and see,' Lady Prescott replied. 'I think you're in for a surprise.'

The blue Rolls Royce pulled __273__ in front of a huge skyscraper that seemed to pierce the clouds. They got out of the car and walked through into the main lobby. Then they made their way to the Managing Director's penthouse suite. As the lift rose smoothly to the eighty-ninth floor, Frederick broke out into a cold sweat.

A thousand thoughts were running __274__ his mind. Could he really trust Lady Prescott? Was he walking into a trap? Would the police be there to arrest him again? And what would Karen Blackstone make __275__ his clothes? He stared at himself in the mirror. He wasn't exactly dressed __276__ for the occasion. In the past twenty-four hours, he'd crawled __277__ mud, swum __278__ lakes, climbed __279__ trees, jumped onto trains, rolled down hills and put a spare wheel onto the blue Rolls Royce. And now, after all that, he looked like a scarecrow in a thunderstorm. The stains on his shirt and his crumpled prison trousers didn't quite fit in with the thick-pile carpet and the soft leather chairs.

When the lift doors opened, they were met by a tall, angular secretary who took one look at Frederick's bedraggled appearance and gave a shrill sniff of disapproval. The woman showed them into the Managing Director's office and sniffed again. Then she turned and closed the door behind her.

◆ ◆ ◆ ◆ ◆ ◆ ◆ ◆ ◆ ◆ ◆ ◆

Chapter Thirteen

Practice

With the introductions over, Karen Blackstone sat down and picked __280__ a pencil.

'Right, let's get down to business,' she said. 'I've been going __281__ your file, Mr Carruthers. As far as I can see, you were a model employee – punctual, industrious, conscientious, loyal. Then came the incident with the kidney machines and you threw away thirty years of hard work. But there are two things in your favour. You know the bank inside out and you're obviously committed to charity work. And that makes you just the person we're looking for.'

'What do you mean?' asked Frederick. 'I don't understand.'

'Then let me explain,' Karen Blackstone said. 'Over the past few months, the bank has run into some problems. For some reason, we've been losing a lot of business. It's a worrying trend. And so – last week – we carried out a survey to find out what's wrong. We discovered, Mr Carruthers, that the bank is not universally loved. It seems that because we don't sponsor operas or football teams or dog shows, people think we're mean. The public sees us as selfish, ruthless and greedy. To put it bluntly, our image puts people __282__

But this can't go __283__ . And so something has to change. I want the bank to come across in a more human, caring way. I want people to look on us as a friend, not as an enemy. I want people to come to us with their problems...'

'... and with their cash!' Frederick said.

Karen Blackstone carried __284__ talking, ignoring that last remark. 'Now, when I heard the story of you and the kidney machines, it set me thinking. We make a solid return on our capital. And it wouldn't do us any harm to give __285__ some of those profits to worthy causes in the community... hospitals, voluntary groups, youth clubs, and so on.

Just think of it, Mr Carruthers. Just think of all the good we could do!'

'And just think of it, Mrs Blackstone,' Frederick said. 'Just think of all that tax-deductible, cheap publicity.'

The Managing Director smiled and then picked __286__ her theme again.

'And this is where you come in, Mr Carruthers. I'd like you to come back to the bank and set the whole thing __287__ . I'm offering you a new job – Head of Charity Donations.'

'And if I was to take up this new challenge,' Frederick said, 'you'd expect me to keep quiet about the events of two years ago. You wouldn't want me to reveal how I showed __288__ the flaws in your security system. In other words, you want to buy my silence.'

Karen Blackstone was drumming her pencil on the table. 'Let's be practical, Mr Carruthers. Not every convict can leave prison and walk straight back into a job. It's very simple. I need you and you need me. It's a case of you scratch my back, I'll scratch yours. I think we understand each other perfectly!'

And so a deal was struck. Frederick got a new job. And Karen Blackstone got a promise that the Head of Charity Donations would never let __289__ how to rip __290__ the bank.

'You'll have your new contract in the morning,' Karen Blackstone said. 'But where shall I send the papers to?'

The question hung in the air like a vulture. It suddenly dawned on Frederick that he couldn't take __291__ a new job until he'd served __292__ his term in jail. And he just didn't know what to say.

Lady Prescott leaned forward. 'If I could just butt in here,' she said. 'I think I've sorted __293__ that problem too. I made two phone calls from the take-away, Mr Carruthers. The first was to Karen, as you know. The second was to my husband. And you'll be leaving prison much sooner than you think.'

◆ ◆ ◆ ◆ ◆ ◆ ◆ ◆ ◆

It was now 5.35 and the blue Rolls Royce was coming home.

'Could you tell me what's going __294__?' Frederick said. 'I'm getting a bit confused.'

'Well, it's all quite simple,' Lady Prescott replied. 'I'm going back to my husband. We had a long talk on the phone and we sorted a few things __295__.'

'But where does that leave me?' Frederick asked. 'Are you going to turn me in?'

'Not exactly.' Lady Prescott smiled. 'I'm going to smuggle you back into the prison and then the governor's going to let you __296__.'

Frederick seemed a bit confused. 'I'm not with you,' he said.

Lady Prescott took a deep breath. 'Gerald tells me that you've served two thirds of your sentence. And since you've been a model prisoner, you're now due for parole. There was no need for you to run off like that. They were going to let you __297__ anyway.'

Frederick was getting lost again.

'Let me put it another way,' Lady Prescott said. 'If you'd stayed in, instead of breaking __298__, the governor would have let you off the last twelve months of your sentence and let you __299__ one year early!'

Frederick's eyebrows collided with each other. The demented goldfish had returned.

Lady Prescott pulled in and stopped the car. 'We'll be there in a few minutes,' she said. 'I've taken a blanket out of the boot. I think it's time for you to hide.'

Frederick had given up trying to work __300__ what was going __301__. So, rather sulkily, he climbed over onto the back seat and covered himself up. A few moments later, the blue Rolls Royce moved __302__ again and headed for Newtown.

By the time they arrived at the prison gates, night was falling. Lady Prescott slowed down and stopped the car. Then she wound down her window and leaned __303__.

◆ ◆ ◆ ◆ ◆ ◆ ◆ ◆ ◆ ◆ ◆ ◆ ◆

CHAPTER FOURTEEN

Practice

'Good evening, Mr Thomas,' she said. 'And how are you tonight?'

The guard smiled. 'I'm fine thanks, Ma'am. We're very glad to see you again.'

He saluted, pressed a button and waved the car through.

The huge iron gates swung open and Lady Prescott drove through into the main prison square. Then she turned down a dimly-lit alley, where she slowed down and parked the car.

She flashed her headlights and Angus – for some reason wearing a false moustache and a pair of dark glasses – came __304__ from behind a large grey dustbin and waved.

Lady Prescott got out of the car and looked __305__. There was no one else about. 'You can come out now, Mr Carruthers,' she whispered. 'The coast is clear. And Mr Macpherson is waiting for you.'

Frederick slipped __306__ of the car and ran down the alley.

'Welcome back, Sir,' Angus said. 'I'm so glad to see you again. I thought I was going to lose my job when you disappeared. I shouldn't have nodded __307__, you see. It was all my fault.'

Frederick smiled and they slipped __308__ a side gate into the main wing of the prison. Angus took the keys off his belt and unlocked cell 269. Then he pushed open the door and stepped back.

'After you, Mr Carruthers,' he said. 'After you.'

Frederick walked into the cell and sat down. 'It feels so strange to be back here,' he said. 'Six hours ago, I was in The Birmingham Big Burger Bar eating a cheeseburger and French fries. Three hours later, I was in the Head Office of the bank. And now I'm here in the darkness of a prison cell. It's been quite a day, Angus. I'll be glad when this whole thing is over and I can get back to my old routine.'

Lady Prescott in the meantime had climbed the steps to the governor's office. Sir Gerald was waiting nervously by the door.

He'd obviously dressed __309__ for the occasion, combing his hair, polishing his shoes and putting __310__ the spotted pink tie that Lady Prescott had given him on their silver wedding anniversary.

History does not record what issues of domestic importance were discussed that evening in the Prescott household. But there is a rumour that the next morning Sir Gerald went out and bought a new pair of rubber washing-__311__ gloves and a book called *How to Flatten Your Stomach and Lose Your Double Chin*.

◆ ◆ ◆ ◆ ◆ ◆ ◆ ◆

That weekend the governor brought the parole forms down to Frederick's cell.

'I owe you a great deal, Mr Carruthers,' he said. 'Your escape was a blessing in disguise. The events of the last twenty-four hours have taught me a lot. I've come to appreciate just how good my life is. Oh, and by the way, my wife has told me all about the kidney machines and the children in the ward. I think you were very brave. I rang up the Home Office last night and we've fixed __312__ your parole. We're going to give you twelve months off for good behaviour!'

That means we'll be letting you **313** on Monday.

　Now, there's just one more thing that we have to sort out. The other prisoners don't know that you escaped. Angus and I hushed the whole thing **314** . So, if anyone asks you where you've been for the past twenty-four hours, just say that we thought you'd gone down with German measles. We took you up to the hospital wing and called in a doctor, but it turned **315** that you had a rash, or an allergy or something, which cleared **316** overnight. You can make **317** any story you like. But don't let on that you managed to break **318** . Otherwise Angus and I will be out of a job.'

　Frederick began to laugh. 'Your secret is safe with me, Governor,' he said. 'And anyway, if anyone found **319** that I ran **320** , I couldn't get parole. So it's in my interests to hush everything **321** too!'

◆ ◆ ◆ ◆ ◆ ◆ ◆ ◆ ◆

Dawn broke over Newtown Prison. It was Monday and Frederick Carruthers was going home. Sir Gerald, Lady Prescott and Angus stood by the front gates to see him off. They shook hands and talked for a few minutes. Then the huge iron gates swung open and Frederick walked out onto the street.

　It was a strange feeling to be truly free again – like having a canvas and a brush and not knowing what to paint. But Frederick was looking forward to doing the simple things again – walking the dogs after Sunday lunch, browsing in bookshops, fishing in the canal.

　The family were there to meet him. They'd stood by him through all the ups and downs of the past two years. And, now, there was so much to say, so much to do. So much lost time to make up **322** .

◆ ◆ ◆ ◆ ◆ ◆ ◆ ◆ ◆

A few days later, a table was reserved at the best Italian restaurant in Newtown. And that night, the Carruthers family, Angus Macpherson and Sir Gerald and Lady Prescott dined out in style.

　There was only one topic of conversation – but that's often the way at the best parties. Frederick told the story of the night of his escape – how he had swum **323** a river, crawled **324** a field of turnips and jumped on and **325** trains. Angus described how he'd broken out into a cold sweat when he'd woken **326** and found **327** that Frederick had managed to break **328** and run **329** . Sir Gerald explained how they'd made **330** a story that Frederick had gone down with a particularly contagious form of German measles in an attempt to hush **331** news of the breakout. And Lady Prescott recounted the story of driving into a lay-by and coming **332** a shabby down-and-out with such a kindly, honest face.

◆ ◆ ◆ ◆ ◆ ◆ ◆ ◆ ◆ ◆ ◆ ◆

CHAPTER FIFTEEN

Practice

At 10.30, just after the fourth course, but some time before the fifth, Angus looked __333__ his watch and sighed.

'I'll have to go now,' he said. 'I'm on duty in half an hour.'

He stood __334__ and said goodbye to Mrs Carruthers, the children, Sir Gerald and Lady Prescott. Then he turned and thanked Frederick for the meal.

'Thank *you*, Angus,' Frederick replied. 'None of this would have been possible if you hadn't let me escape. You've changed my life. I owe you a lot.'

Angus blushed a deep shade of red and looked down at the floor. 'All's well that ends well,' he said, doing __335__ his coat. Frederick smiled and patted him on the shoulder.

Angus left the restaurant and walked back along the peaceful streets of Newtown. When he came to the prison gates, he knocked on the front door and the night guard let him in. Angus clocked on, put on his uniform, and then went through the corridors checking the cells and turning off the lights.

Everything was in order. The prisoners had settled down for the night and the jail was locked and still.

Angus yawned and sat down on a small wooden bench. He was tired. And now – as the clock struck eleven – the French fries, the Welsh rabbit made with blue cheese, the Scotch egg covered with French dressing, the steak (well done) and the three platefuls of spaghetti bolognese he'd enjoyed at dinner were pulling him towards the deepest of deep sleeps.

'I'll just have a little nap,' he thought to himself. 'I'm sure nobody will mind if I nod off for a while.'

He stretched out, took off his belt and dropped it onto the floor.

A few minutes later, the stone corridors echoed to Angus Macpherson's unmistakable snores.

Meanwhile, in the darkness of cell 269, Angela Richardson, (an athlete who had run off with the membership fees of her local sports club) was planning her escape.

But that – as they say – is another story...

◆ ◆ ◆ ◆ ◆ ◆ ◆ ◆ ◆ ◆ ◆ ◆ ◆ ◆

ANSWERS

Vocabulary Exercises

Exercise 1

1 belt
2 floor
3 keys
4 door
5 yard
6 wall
7 breakfast
8 cell
9 breath
10 bars

Exercise 2

1 off
2 over
3 to
4 off
5 out
6 across
7 over
8 around
9 about
10 up

Exercise 3

1 belt
2 desk
3 cell
4 minutes
5 keys
6 door
7 *Times*
8 tears
9 handkerchief
10 lunchbreak

Exercise 4

1 for
2 at
3 with
4 out
5 away
6 off
7 up
8 out
9 to
10 off

Exercise 5

1 coat
2 prisoners
3 tears
4 nonsense
5 marriage
6 coat
7 breakdown
8 door
9 pounds
10 patience

Exercise 6

1 off
2 up
3 away
4 into
5 of
6 with
7 up
8 on
9 about
10 out

Exercise 7

1 tears
2 weight
3 jogging
4 smoking
5 dinner
6 chair
7 room
8 tie
9 women
10 handkerchief

Exercise 8

1 on
2 out
3 away
4 round
5 over
6 out
7 after
8 down
9 up
10 out

Exercise 9 (Revision)

1 Angus
2 Angus
3 Sir Gerald
4 Angus
5 Angus (Chapter Two),
  Sir Gerald (Chapter Four)
6 Frederick
7 Sir Gerald
8 Sir Gerald
9 Lady Prescott
10 Lady Prescott
11 Sir Gerald
12 Lady Prescott
13 Lady Prescott
14 Sir Gerald
15 Frederick
16 Frederick
17 Frederick
18 Frederick
19 Frederick
20 Lady Prescott

Exercise 10

1 window
2 tyre
3 glass
4 jacket
5 hand
6 cloth
7 seat belt
8 handbrake
9 mirror
10 lay-by

Exercise 11

1 over
2 out
3 up
4 out
5 off
6 on
7 in
8 on
9 off
10 onto

Exercise 12

1 name
2 spine
3 reputation
4 kitten
5 wall
6 sounds

7 subject
8 volcano
9 Rolls Royce
10 prison

Exercise 13

1 to
2 across
3 of
4 for
5 in
6 through
7 out
8 up
9 back
10 on

Exercise 14

1 street
2 handbrake
3 seat belt
4 houses
5 childhood
6 workaholic
7 spine
8 love
9 mind
10 Gerald

Exercise 15

1 at
2 on
3 up
4 around
5 up
6 round
7 out
8 out
9 on
10 out

Exercise 16

1 proposing
2 key
3 back
4 phone
5 money
6 cheek
7 penny
8 way
9 complaints
10 husband

Exercise 17

1 at
2 through
3 on
4 to
5 out
6 on
7 at
8 to
9 out
10 with

Exercise 18 (Revision)

1 Frederick
2 Frederick
3 Lady Prescott
4 Lady Prescott
5 Frederick
6 Lady Prescott
7 Lady Prescott
8 Lady Prescott
9 Lady Prescott
10 Lady Prescott
11 Sir Gerald
12 Sir Gerald
13 Lady Prescott
14 Lady Prescott
15 Lady Prescott's father
16 Lady Prescott
17 Sir Gerald and Lady Prescott
18 Lady Prescott's father
19 Lady Prescott
20 Frederick

Exercise 19

1 cheque
2 payments
3 story
4 account
5 police
6 office
7 jail
8 bank
9 hand
10 trial

Exercise 20

1 to
2 in
3 through
4 for
5 of
6 in
7 for
8 of
9 with
10 up

Exercise 21

1 prison
2 diary
3 number
4 people
5 hours
6 start
7 surprise
8 mind
9 clothes
10 office

Exercise 22

1 off
2 of
3 with
4 apart
5 up
6 out
7 up
8 to
9 for
10 of

Exercise 23

1 pencil
2 file
3 survey
4 image
5 friend
6 profits
7 Frederick
8 job
9 jail
10 problem

Exercise 24

1 through
2 out
3 out
4 as
5 off
6 to
7 out
8 up
9 out
10 on

Exercise 25

1 coast
2 belt
3 life
4 behaviour
5 rash
6 parole
7 river
8 trains
9 Frederick
10 breakout

Exercise 26

1 off
2 on
3 out
4 out
5 away
6 up
7 out
8 of
9 across
10 on

Exercise 27 (Revision)

1 Frederick
2 Lady Prescott
3 Frederick
4 Frederick
5 Frederick
6 Karen Blackstone
7 Frederick
8 Frederick
9 Lady Prescott
10 Frederick
11 Angus
12 Angus
13 Frederick (Chapter Fourteen),
Angus (Chapter Fifteen)
14 Sir Gerald
15 Angus
16 Angus
17 Angus
18 Angus
19 Angus
20 Angus

Cloze Test

Chapter One

1 off
2 out
3 over
4 off
5 onto
6 off
7 out
8 across
9 over
10 on
11 around
12 about
13 out
14 up

Chapter Two

15 up
16 for
17 out
18 up
19 at
20 in
21 in
22 down
23 through
24 out
25 off
26 off
27 up
28 up
29 into
30 off
31 off
32 for
33 up
34 for
35 out

Chapter Three

36 off
37 up
38 into
39 on
40 with
41 away
42 down
43 after
44 down
45 after
46 down
47 after

48 over
49 into
50 up
51 away
52 down
53 about
54 after
55 over
56 into
57 out

Chapter Four

58 into
59 on
60 up
61 off
62 up
63 up
64 round
65 at
66 over
67 out
68 up
69 up
70 away
71 down
72 down
73 into
74 up
75 out
76 into

Chapter Five

77 out
78 out
79 across
80 through
81 through
82 across
83 off
84 off
85 through
86 through
87 through
88 out
89 on
90 through

Chapter Six

91 across
92 out
93 out
94 off
95 off

96 on
97 out
98 on
99 on
100 out
101 onto

Chapter Seven

102 on
103 across
104 out
105 of
106 down
107 of
108 into
109 into
110 up
111 back
112 in
113 from
114 on

Chapter Eight

115 down
116 up
117 on
118 down
119 up
120 down
121 up
122 down
123 back
124 up
125 on
126 off
127 out
128 around
129 off
130 over
131 up
132 down
133 apart
134 round
135 on
136 down
137 round
138 down
139 up
140 down
141 away
142 into
143 in
144 at
145 down

146 out

147 on

148 to

149 up

150 in

151 out

152 on

153 out

154 up

155 on

156 up

157 up

158 out

159 up

160 through

161 on

162 in

163 out

164 up

165 up

166 off

167 on

168 down

169 up

Chapter Nine

170 down

171 down

172 through

173 on

174 on

175 out

176 down

177 off

178 to

179 out

180 in

181 up

182 in

183 on

184 out

185 away

186 away

187 through

188 round

189 out

190 up

191 through

192 up

193 up

194 into

195 on

196 up

197 for

198 on

199 out

200 up

Chapter Ten

201 at

202 on

203 around

204 up

205 around

206 out

207 in

208 around

209 off

210 up

211 off

212 after

213 through

214 across

215 up

216 out

217 around

218 up

219 up

220 through

221 up

Chapter Eleven

222 at

223 up

224 about

225 up

226 on

227 out

228 up

229 up

230 on

231 through

232 up

233 out

234 up

235 off

236 apart

237 over

238 off

239 through

240 at

241 up

242 through

243 up

244 up

Chapter Twelve

245 out

246 off

247 apart
248 up
249 up
250 up
251 out
252 up
253 round
254 up
255 through
256 back
257 up
258 up
259 off
260 up
261 out
262 up
263 up
264 off
265 on
266 off
267 up
268 up
269 out
270 off
271 up
272 up
273 up
274 through
275 of
276 up
277 through
278 across
279 up

Chapter Thirteen

280 up
281 through
282 off
283 on
284 on
285 away
286 up
287 up
288 up
289 on
290 off
291 up
292 out
293 out
294 on
295 out
296 out
297 out
298 out
299 out

300 out
301 on
302 off
303 across

Chapter Fourteen

304 out
305 around
306 out
307 off
308 through
309 up
310 on
311 up
312 up
313 out
314 up
315 out
316 up
317 up
318 out
319 out
320 away
321 up
322 for
323 across
324 through
325 off
326 up
327 out
328 out
329 away
330 up
331 up
332 across

Chapter Fifteen

333 at
334 up
335 up

PHRASAL VERB LIST

ask about	The next morning, I rang up the hospital to ask about the little boy.	10
ask out	One afternoon, he asked me out and we went for a walk in the park.	8
bang on	With his heart pounding, he banged on the door.	2
be about	There were now lots of people about.	12
be back	I could slip out through the side door, run across the yard, jump over the prison wall and be back home for breakfast.	1
be in for	I think you are in for a surprise.	12
be off	I've run out of patience. I'm off.	3
be over	When the film was over, we caught the last bus home.	9
be up to	My father seemed happy, but he didn't know what I was really up to.	8
be with	Frederick seemed a bit confused. 'I'm not with you,' he said.	13
bend down	Frederick bent down and ran his hand over the tyre.	6
blow up	She blows up all the time.	4
board up	It's dirty and messy and some of the shops are boarded up.	8
bottle up	You shouldn't just bottle it up inside you.	10
breakdown	If you run away to a run-down area of Birmingham, I'll have a nervous breakdown.	3
break down	The bus broke down and all the passengers had to get off and walk.	9
break off	Lady Prescott broke off and – once again – they walked on in silence.	9
break out into	Frederick broke out into a cold sweat.	12
break out of	He's broken out of his cell and run away.	2
break up	It was half past three and the local school had just broken up for the day.	12
break up	I'm going to break up our marriage and run away to a run-down area of Birmingham.	3
break up with	I said that I'd broken up with Gerald.	8
bring back	Telling the story of the kidney machines had brought back some painful memories.	12
build up	She noticed that I'd been building up large amounts of cash.	11
burst into	Sir Gerald took a handkerchief out of his pocket, blew his nose and, not for the first time, burst into tears.	4
bust-up	After my bust-up with Sir Gerald, I just needed someone to talk to.	10
butt in	Lady Prescott leaned forward. 'If I could just butt in here,' she said.	13
call in	We took you up to the hospital wing and called in a doctor.	14

call into	One afternoon, I called my secretary into the office.	10
calm down	'Now calm down,' Sir Gerald said. 'And go through the whole story very slowly right from the start.'	2
care about	Money! Money! Money! That's all you care about.	3
carry away	Lady Prescott was getting carried away and there was just no stopping her now.	7
carry out	We carried out a survey.	13
catch up with	The last twenty-four hours were beginning to catch up with him.	12
check up on	Nobody checked up on what I was doing.	10
cheer up	Oh, and do cheer up, Mr Carruthers. You mustn't worry so much.	12
clear out	I'll clear out the cupboards and take you out at the weekends.	4
clear up	It turned out that you had a rash, or an allergy or something, which cleared up overnight.	14
climb up	Frederick...climbed up a hill.	5
climb over	He had climbed over a couple of gates.	5
clock on	Angus clocked on, put on his uniform and then went through the corridors, checking the cells and turning off the lights.	15
come across	I'm sure I've come across it somewhere before.	7
come along	'Come along, Mr Carruthers!' Lady Prescott said. 'Wake up. We're nearly there.'	12
come back	Whenever I feel down, I come back here.	8
come in	'Come in,' he shouted. 'The door's open.'	2
come in	And this is where you come in, Mr Carruthers.	13
come out	'You can come out now, Mr Carruthers,' she whispered. 'The coast is clear.'	14
come out	He did manage a few incoherent grunts, but none of the sounds came out right.	7
come out from	Angus came out from behind a large, grey dustbin and waved.	14
come round	Whenever there's an election, the politicians come round and knock on the door.	8
come to	When he came to the prison gates, he knocked on the front door and the night guard let him in.	15
come to	I trust you've come to your senses.	11
come up with	Then – all of a sudden – I came up with an idea.	10
come upon	They came upon a postman riding a bicycle.	9
crash onto	They crashed noisily onto the floor and rolled under my bed.	11
crawl through	Frederick...crawled through a field full of turnips.	5
cry out	His stomach was crying out for food and his throat felt like sandpaper.	5

dawn on	Gradually, shockingly, horrifyingly, the awful truth dawned on him.	2
dine out	And that night, the Carruthers family, Angus Macpherson and Sir Gerald and Lady Prescott dined out in style.	14
dive into	Frederick had dived into a stream and swum across to the opposite bank.	5
do up	'All's well that ends well,' he said, doing up his coat.	15
do up	They've done up some of the houses, but most of the properties are falling down or falling apart.	8
down-and-out	You were standing around with your hands in your pockets looking like a down-and-out.	10
drag back	Lady Prescott turned round and dragged him back inside.	12
draw up	The blue Rolls Royce slowed down and they drew up in front of a row of shabby, terraced houses.	8
dress up	Sir Gerald...had obviously dressed up for the occasion, combing his hair, polishing his shoes and putting on the spotted pink tie that Lady Prescott had given him on their silver wedding anniversary.	14
drift around	It is strange that I was drifting around with nowhere to go.	10
drink up	Frederick drank up his coffee, ate up his cheeseburger, finished off his French fries and then stood up.	12
drive down to	One day I drove down to the hospital to pick my mother up after work.	10
drive into	When I drove into that lay-by, you were standing around with your hands in your pockets.	10
drop off	I'm going to Birmingham. Perhaps I can drop you off somewhere along the way.	6
drop onto	He rolled over, took off the belt and dropped it onto the floor.	1
eat up	Frederick drank up his coffee, ate up his cheeseburger, finished off his French fries and then stood up.	12
echo to	A few minutes later, the stone corridors echoed to Angus Macpherson's unmistakable snore.	1
end up	He ended up standing outside a cafe in a lay-by near Junction 34 of the M1 motorway.	5
explain away	I made up some new story to explain the cheques away.	11
fall apart	They've done up some of the houses, but most of the properties are falling down or falling apart.	8
fall down	They've done up some of the houses, but most of the properties are falling down or falling apart.	8
fall out	The man from the bank gaped at me and his false teeth fell out.	11
fall for	She fell for it every time.	11
feel down	Whenever I feel down, I come back here.	8
find out	When my father found out what was going on, he went crazy.	8

finish off	Frederick drank up his coffee, ate up his cheeseburger, finished off his French fries and then stood up.	12
fit in with	The stains on his shirt and his crumpled prison trousers didn't quite fit in with the thick-pile carpet and the soft leather chairs.	12
fix up	When we were in the take-away, I rang up your Head Office and fixed up an appointment with Karen Blackstone.	12
fold up	I took a deep breath, folded up the cheque and put it into my pocket.	11
get away with	Could I get away with it?	11
get back to	I'll be glad when this whole thing is over and I can get back to my old routine.	14
get carried away	And I suppose I got a bit carried away.	11
get down to	'Right, let's get down to business,' she said.	13
get in	The woman got in, put on her seat belt and looked in the rear-view mirror.	6
get in	That night, he'd decided to stay up until I got in.	9
get into	'That's very kind of you,' he said, wiping his hands on a cloth and getting into the car.	6
get into	I don't know what's got into her lately.	4
get into	How did I get into this mess?	5
get off	…the other passengers were getting off the train.	5
get off	If I could get the keys off Macpherson's belt…	1
get off to sleep	But, for some reason, he couldn't get off to sleep.	1
get on	We got on really well and I started seeing him all the time.	8
get out of	How do I get out of this mess?	5
get out of	I might have got out of going to prison, but what would have happened to the children?	12
get out of	Lady Prescott got out of the car and looked around.	14
get round to	But when the votes are counted, they never seem to get round to it.	8
give away	…it wouldn't do us any harm to give away some of those profits to worthy causes in the community.	13
give in	He thought I was going to give in without a fight.	11
give up	I'll give up smoking and wash up after dinner.	4
give up	I knew that I couldn't give Gerald up.	8
go after	'Shall I go after her?' Angus asked, from somewhere behind the armchair.	4
go ahead	And so the trial went ahead.	11
go away	If you went away, I'd go to pieces.	4
go back on	I'm not going back on my word.	11
go down with	We thought you'd gone down with German measles.	14
go for	He asked me out and we went for a walk in the park.	8
go in	One day, I went in to get some chips.	8
go into	One morning, I didn't go into work.	11

go on	Or should I defy my parents and go on seeing him?	8
go on	She went on like a dragon breathing fire.	7
go on	When my father found out what was going on, he went crazy.	8
go on	'Go on,' Lady Prescott said gently.	10
go on	And so it went on.	11
go out	I went out in rather a hurry last night.	9
go out of	You've gone out of your way to help me.	9
go out to	Then one night, we went out to the cinema.	9
go out with	He didn't want his only daughter going out with someone who cooked hamburgers in a take-away.	8
go over	I went over it again and again.	11
go round to	I went straight round to Gerald's flat and we decided to run away.	9
go through	'Now calm down,' Sir Gerald said. 'And go through the whole story very slowly right from the start.'	2
go through	For the next few months, we went through a really bad patch.	9
go through	They went through my account.	11
go through	Angus clocked on, put on his uniform and then went through the corridors, checking the cells and turning off the lights.	15
go through	I cried for two or three days and went through ten packets of tissues.	8
go through with	I've decided to go through with the trial.	11
go to	I went to the hospital to pick my mother up after work.	10
grow up	And this little run-down street on the edge of the city is where I grew up.	8
hand back	I bent down, picked them up and handed them back to him.	11
hand to	Angus took a handkerchief out of his pocket and handed it to Sir Gerald.	2
hang up	Frederick took off his jacket and hung it up on one of the wing mirrors.	6
hard up	He was so hard up that he'd use the same tea bag for a week.	9
have on	I'm afraid I don't have any money on me.	9
head for	But this was no dream. And their car was heading straight for the main entrance.	12
hear of	Perhaps you've heard of him. His name is Sir Gerald Prescott.	7
hold out	Frederick nodded, smiled and held out his hand.	6
hold up	His trousers were held up with string.	9
hold up	Then he pulled a large piece of glass out of the tyre and held it up.	6
hunt down	And we will hunt you down until we get every penny of our money back.	11

hush up	Angus and I hushed the whole thing up.	14
jack up	Frederick took off his jacket, jacked up the car, took off the flat tyre and put on the spare wheel.	6
jump off	Frederick jumped off as the train pulled into a station.	5
jump onto	Frederick jumped onto a train that was slowing down in front of a set of signals.	5
jump over	I could slip out through the side door, run across the yard, jump over the prison wall and be back home for breakfast.	1
keep on	Gerald kept on proposing and I kept on saying 'no'.	9
kneel down	'You can't do this to me,' the prison governor shouted, kneeling down and bursting into tears.	4
knock down	I'd be a bit sad if they knocked everything down and put up one of those ugly tower blocks.	8
knock on	When he came to the prison, he knocked on the front door and the night guard let him in.	15
knock over	Lady Prescott turned round, threw an ashtray at Sir Gerald, knocked over a chair and stormed out of the room.	4
know about	Do you know anything about cars?	6
know of	I know of him... He has quite a reputation in my field.	7
lay-by	He ended up standing outside a café in a lay-by near Junction 34 of the M1 motorway.	5
lean across	The driver wound down her window and leaned across.	6
let down	I can't let the children down.	11
let in	When he came to the prison, he knocked on the front door and the night guard let him in.	15
let on	...but just don't let on that you managed to break out.	14
let off	They might even have let you off.	12
let out	Stop the car right now. Let me out!	12
let through	I'm a train engineer. Let me through.	5
lie against	He had to lie against pillows all day long.	10
look across	I looked across and saw a little boy.	10
look after	She looks after sick children.	10
look around	Lady Prescott got out of the car and looked around.	14
look at	I looked at the cheque. My head was spinning.	11
look back	I suppose that now – looking back – I can appreciate what my parents were going through.	9
look down	Angus blushed a deep shade of red and looked down at the floor.	15
look for	Angus stood up and looked for his belt.	2
look in	The woman got in, put on her seat belt and looked in the rear-view mirror.	6
look on as	I want people to look on us as a friend, not an enemy.	13
look out of	Frederick looked out of the window and waved his hand in a rather vague way.	7
look through	Frederick looked through the windows of the café.	5

look up	Frederick looked up. 'You're right, of course,' he said, breaking the silence.	10
look up	She took a yellow diary out of the bag and looked up a number.	12
make out	I can't understand women, Angus. I just can't make them out.	4
make up your mind	She's made up her mind to run away to a run-down area of Birmingham and there's nothing we can do.	4
make up	I made up some story or other to explain where I'd been.	8
make up	I made it up with my parents.	9
make up for	Give me one last chance. I'll make up for it.	4
move off	The blue Rolls Royce moved off and headed for Newtown.	13
move on to	Frederick wanted to move on to another topic like the weather or the price of cauliflowers.	7
nod off	I'm sure nobody will mind if I nod off for a while.	1
open up	He walked to the back of the car and opened up the boot.	6
pass through	I was a bank manager and a lot of money passed through my hands.	10
pay back	Paying for lunch will be my way of paying you back for all your kindness.	9
pay for	Paying for lunch will be my way of paying you back for all your kindness.	9
pay off	After two years in jail, you've paid off your debt.	12
pick up	He stretched out his hand, picked up the belt and lifted it back through the bars.	1
pick up	I went to the hospital to pick my mother up after work.	10
pick up	Frederick took a deep breath and picked up the story again.	10
pick up	You must have picked it up along the way.	6
plug in	I unwrapped the machines, plugged them in and switched them on.	11
pop in	Why don't we pop in here and have a late lunch?	9
pull down	They promise to pull down the terraced housing and build some new flats.	8
pull in	Lady Prescott pulled in and stopped the car.	13
pull into	Frederick jumped off as the train pulled into a station.	5
pull into	…a blue Rolls Royce pulled into the lay-by and glided to a halt.	5
pull out	Then he pulled a large piece of glass out of the tyre and held it up.	6
pull out	She pulled gently out of the lay-by.	6
pull up	The blue Rolls Royce slowed down and they pulled up in front of a shabby terraced house.	8
pump up	Frederick put on the spare wheel and pumped it up a little.	6
put away	Put the letter away. I've got no intention of signing it.	11

put back	'No,' Sir Gerald replied softly, picking up the ashtray and putting it back on the table.	4
put down	When I put down the phone, I felt terribly disturbed.	10
put down	…the driver put her foot down and the blue Rolls Royce roared on.	7
put into	The woman took off the handbrake, looked in the rear-view mirror and put the car into first gear.	6
put into	'Try the beginning,' said Lady Prescott, putting a straw into her milkshake.	10
put off	To put it bluntly, our image puts people off.	13
put on	'That's it,' Lady Prescott said, putting on her coat. 'I've had enough of all this nonsense.'	3
put on	…put on her seat belt…	6
put on	…put on the spare wheel…	6
put on	Lady Prescott put on the handbrake, took off her seat belt and stepped out of the car.	8
put on	I've been working too hard and putting on weight.	4
put on	I put on a really good show.	8
put up	I'd be a bit sad if they…put up one of those ugly tower blocks.	8
put up with	I hate to see a grown man cry and I'm not going to put up with it any longer.	3
rabbit on	I've been rabbiting on about my problems for over an hour now.	10
ride across	And as he rode across the cobblestones, he seemed to be nodding his head and shaking his head at the same time.	9
ring up	The next morning, I rang up the hospital to ask about the little boy.	10
rip off	You can't rip the bank off and expect to get away with it.	11
roar onto	She pulled gently out of the lay-by and then – with a sudden burst of speed – roared onto the M1 motorway like a bullet from a gun.	6
roll down	Frederick…rolled down a hill.	5
roll over	He rolled over, took off the belt and dropped it onto the floor.	1
run across	I could slip out through the side door, run across the yard, jump over the prison wall and be back home for breakfast.	1
run after	If you run away, I'll run after you.	3
run away	I'm going to break up our marriage and run away to a run-down area of Birmingham.	3
run-down	She's made up her mind to run off to a run-down area of Birmingham and there's nothing we can do.	4
run down	He smiled at me and I felt a cold shiver run down my spine.	8
run down	Frederick had…run down the corridor to avoid the ticket collector.	5

run into	The bank has run into some problems.	13
run into	If you run away to a run-down area and I run after you and you run over me in our car, you might then run into a tree and the cost of repairing the damage might run into hundreds of pounds.	3
run off	She's made up her mind to run off to a run-down area of Birmingham and there's nothing we can do.	4
run out of	I've run out of patience. I'm off.	3
run over	Frederick bent down and ran his hand over the tyre.	6
run over	If you run away to a run-down area and I run after you and you run over me in our car, you might then run into a tree…	3
run through	These were the thoughts running through Frederick Carruthers' troubled mind as a blue Rolls Royce pulled into the lay-by and glided to a halt.	5
run up	Angus ran up the steps to the prison governor's office.	2
rush down	Angus…rushed down the corridor.	2
rush in	Angus rushed in, his red face covered with sweat.	2
save up	By that summer, I'd managed to save up a quarter of a million pounds.	11
see as	The public sees us as selfish, ruthless and greedy.	13
see off	Sir Gerald, Lady Prescott and Angus stood by the front gate to see him off.	14
send back	Just tell them to send the machines back.	11
serve out	It suddenly dawned on Frederick that he couldn't take up a new job until he'd served out his term in jail.	13
set off	Lady Prescott locked the car and they set off across the market square.	8
set up	This is the Head Office of the bank. You've set me up, haven't you?	12
set up	I'd like you to come back to the bank and set the whole thing up.	13
settle down	I told him I was just too young to settle down.	9
settle down	The prisoners had settled down for the night and the jail was locked and still.	15
show around	And now, Mr Carruthers, I'm going for a walk. Would you like me to show you around?	8
show up	I showed up the flaws in your security system.	13
sit at	Sir Gerald was sitting at his desk reading *The Times*.	2
sit back	Frederick sat back and watched the volcano erupt.	7
sit down	Angus sat down and took a deep breath.	2
sit in	Frederick was sitting in a Rolls Royce driven by the wife of the governor of the prison he had just escaped from.	7
sit up	He was so ill that he couldn't sit up in bed properly.	10
slam down	He lost his temper and slammed down the phone.	9
slip out	I could slip out through the side door, run across the yard, jump over the prison wall and be back home for breakfast.	1

slip through	Frederick slipped through the ticket barrier by showing his prison identification badge.	5
slow down	Frederick jumped onto a train that was slowing down in front of a set of signals.	5
sort out	There's just one more thing that we have to sort out.	14
split up	Should I obey my father and split up with the person I loved?	8
speed on	The blue Rolls Royce sped on towards Birmingham.	7
stand around	When I drove into that lay-by, you were standing around with your hands in your pockets.	10
stand by	I couldn't stand by and do nothing.	10
stand by	They'd stood by him through all the ups and downs of the past two years.	14
stand up	Angus stood up and looked for his belt.	2
stay in	If you'd stayed in instead of breaking out, the governor would have...let you out one year early!	13
stay up	He normally went to bed at about eleven, but that night he had decided to stay up until I got in.	9
step back	Then he pushed open the door and stepped back.	14
step out of	Lady Prescott put on the handbrake, took off her seat belt and stepped out of the car.	8
stretch out	Angus stretched out on a wooden bench and tried to relax.	1
storm out of	Lady Prescott turned round, threw an ashtray at Sir Gerald, knocked over a chair and stormed out of the room.	4
swim across	Frederick had...swum across to the opposite bank.	5
switch on	...plugged them in and switched them on...	11
take-away	He'd taken a part-time job at a take-away restaurant called The Birmingham Big Burger Bar.	8
take in	My parents were completely taken in.	8
take off	He rolled over, took off the belt and dropped it onto the floor.	1
take off	I'll take up jogging and take off weight.	4
take on	The bank would never dream of taking me on again.	12
take out	I'll clear out the cupboards and take you out at weekends.	4
take out	Sir Gerald took a handkerchief out of his pocket, blew his nose and, not for the first time, burst into tears.	4
take up	I'll take up jogging and take off weight.	4
take up	And if I was to take up this new challenge...	13
talk to	I needed someone to talk to.	10
tear down	I don't want them tearing down my childhood.	8
tear up	'But that's terrible,' the prison governor screamed, tearing up his *Times* and bursting into tears.	2
think over	We're going to give you twenty-four hours to think it over.	11
think through	He had to give me more time to think things through.	9

throw at	Lady Prescott turned round, threw an ashtray at Sir Gerald, knocked over a chair and stormed out of the room.	4
throw away	Should I just tear up the cheque and throw it away?	11
tip off	She tipped off the police, and when I turned up for work the next morning, there were three detectives waiting in my office.	11
tire out	I'm tired out and very worked up about my husband.	9
turn round	Lady Prescott turned round, threw an ashtray at Sir Gerald, knocked over a chair and stormed out of the room.	4
turn down	I felt very flattered, but at first I always turned him down.	9
turn down	…as they turned down a narrow side street, Lady Prescott picked up the story again.	8
turn in	If she found out that he was a convict on the run, perhaps she would turn him in.	10
turn into	…as they turned into the main road…	9
turn into	It's only recently that he's turned into a workaholic who eats, drinks and sleeps prisons.	8
turn out	…but it turned out that you had a rash, or an allergy or something, which cleared up overnight.	14
turn off*	Angus clocked on, put on his uniform and then went through the corridors checking the cells and turning off the lights.	15
turn out*	… Angus had turned out the light in his cell.	5
turn up	When I turned up for work the next morning, there were three detectives waiting in my office.	11
wade through	Frederick had…waded through a swamp…	5
wait for	My father was waiting for me in the hall.	9
wake up	Frederick woke up with a start.	12
walk around	Then the children would be able to get out of bed and walk around the ward.	10
walk into	I walked into the hospital and wrote out a cheque for £250,000.	11
walk into	Was I walking into a trap?	12
walk on	They walked on in silence.	9
walk out of	I'm going to walk out of that door and you'll never see me again.	3
walk out on	You can't walk out on me like this.	4
walk over to	Lady Prescott walked over to the pay-phone in the corner of the room.	12
walk through	As I was walking through one of the wards, I could hear a child crying very softly.	10
wander around	Why were you wandering around near the motorway with no money in your pocket and those very strange clothes?	10

* In these two sentences, *turn out* and *turn off* have the same meaning.

warm to	Lady Prescott's voice grew louder as she warmed to her subject.	7
wash up	I'll give up smoking and wash up after dinner.	4
wave through	The guard saluted, pressed a button and waved the car through.	14
wind down	The driver wound down her window and leaned across.	6
work out	When Angus had at last worked out what had happened, he rushed down the corridor and ran up the steps to the prison governor's office.	2
wrap up in	I've been so wrapped up in my work that I've started to take you for granted.	4